Published by MM, Cheltenham, England
Website: www.mmpublish.org
Contact: mmp@gmx.com

Book Cover by Jessica Bell Design
Portrait photo by Grace Portraits

First edition 2023

ISBN 978-1-916616-00-4 (pbk)

ISBN 978-1-916616-01-1 (ebook)

CONTENTS

FOREWORD

I have been privileged to know Kevin for more than 25 years and I am one of countless people inspired by his tireless and faithful love and discipleship. There are not many people who can combine being a nuclear engineer, family man, youth worker, event organiser and DJ, but he managed it.

He has always been a "boots on the ground" Christian, sharing God's love practically and creatively with people in his local community. This inspiring book explains how God has worked through Kevin's whole life and has now called him again to mission overseas.

Kevin combines the ordinary with the extraordinary, the epic with the intimate and through this book reminds us - especially us cynical Christians worn down by the world - that the love of Jesus still has the same miraculous power that it ever did.

This is a brilliant book by an inspiring man. 'See Miracles' is the story of a Christian who has simply tried to be open to the power of Jesus and has seen our Saviour work powerfully in and through him.

Kevin brings the comfort and challenge that Jesus can work miracles in and through any of us, and gives us the tools to help make it a reality.

This book manages to make the miraculous and the spiritual feel earthy and tangible and real, just as it was in the New Testament.

A timely challenge to shake me out of my comfortable Christianity.

DAVID WATERS, ***Senior Producer, BBC Songs of Praise***

SEE MIRACLES

LET'S GO EXPLORING

Do you like exploring? Going on an adventure, where you're not sure what's round the next corner. Where what you experience stands out sharp and new, so you're learning all the time. And what you learn might change the rest of your life.

Are you up for it? If so, come and walk through these pages. Our journey starts in a European country like no other, but it's really a journey into the Kingdom of God, the seen and unseen world that overlaps every country on Earth, where God does miracles every day, where he definitely wants you to get involved. In fact, it's where he invites you to live.

So.... first stop: North Macedonia, a country right on the fringes of Europe. Meet the people of this wild, exciting land and begin to share my passion. Maybe God will call you to pray for it. One day you may even go and support his church there. If so, you'll be following the Apostle Paul, whose vision of the "man of Macedonia"[1] took him there nearly 2000 years ago. Just as the Holy Spirit performed miracles through Paul in Philippi and elsewhere, you'll see astonishing miracles in North Macedonia today.

Later on, we will fly off to East Africa to see some miracles there, but we will also be spending time at home; God's Kingdom is everywhere. We just need to learn to see it. The miracles God is doing in Macedonia and Africa, he's doing in your country too. His invitation is here and now. He has much more to give you than you maybe realise: closeness to him, gifts and challenges too.

It's time to start our journey...

A European country like no other

A woman sits on the bare floor of her house. In front of her is a 25kg bag of flour, a bottle of cooking oil, a few other basic essentials like lentils and dried beans, a can of fish, and a packet of biscuits. The food parcel will be enough to feed her and her family for a month, just.

She is not in drought-afflicted East Africa, or a refugee from the Middle East conflict. This is a Roma lady, suffering poverty in Europe whilst fuel and food prices rocket. As I write this, her family are eking out their lives on that donation from our UK charity.

Nearby, is a rickety building the size of a garage in a British or American home. The gable wall had partly collapsed so there was no protection from bitter winter winds. The grandmother has recently died, but a family of 8 still lives there. Now, though, the local church has stepped in. Repairs are completed and firewood provided. God is at work.

It's Easter. Men, women and children, 230 of them from all over the country, are crammed onto a third-floor balcony worshipping God. The 4-storey building acting now as the church HQ had been bought for half the normal price. It was too haunted for anyone else to want it. The evil spirits arrived when a baby had been killed there; it was deformed, unwanted. Before the church could move in, we had to kick out the evil spirits.

Now, three years later the building is filled with lively singing. The Easter Nova Nadezh (New Hope) celebration has drawn people from all over North Macedonia, driving for hours to get here in well-worn minibuses. People are becoming Christians. A young father, who is a church leader, describes the brain bleed that should have killed him a few weeks earlier, had God not intervened. People keep on coming forward. They are being healed from physical illnesses, addictions and mental issues, or meeting their Saviour for the first time.

"The blind receive sight, the lame walk... the deaf hear... and the good news is preached to the poor."[2] It's happening here, now.

It may sound incredible, but it is real, and this journey of spiritual discovery is for each of us. We start from exactly where we are, and take one step at a time into what Jesus has for our lives. This book is not for or about spiritual superstars. It is for the everyday follower of Jesus, who wants to go deeper into the adventure that God has for us, starting from exactly where we are.

Turn the page. Let's explore the Kingdom and be open to whatever God says and does. See how great our God is... And learn to see miracles...

References

1. Acts 16:9

2. Luke 7:22

MIRACLES ARE...

Miracles are... God doing things unexpectedly

God is doing things all the time: the universe could not exist even for a second without him holding it all together.[1] But because he *is* doing it all the time, we generally fail to notice. God's unexpected actions are not more important than his everyday ones; we just notice them more.

The greatest and most common miracles happen when you realise how hungry you are for God, and God reaches in, to you, the incredibly complicated, beautiful, damaged person that you are, and starts to rearrange and heal and pour in his love.

Since you've picked up this book, the chances are that you have experienced this greatest of miracles already; if you haven't, I am sure that you will. God never makes mistakes. You have picked up this book for a reason. He always knows what he is doing.

Right from the opening pages, you'll see people being healed. God's miracles will always surprise us. And (especially if we live in the cynical West) supernatural healing will always take our breath away.

But physical healing is not the only sort of miracle. It's not even the only sort of *healing*.

An Olympic athlete who is blind to God is less healthy, the Bible explains, than a blind girl who is full of love for God and for others. The term in the Bible that is closest to our word "health" is *Shalom,* but it includes so much more richness and depth. It's about being restored to the person we were always meant to be, in right relationship with God,

with others,

with our mind,

our body,

our spirit.

The choice: love or staying numb

The bedrock of Shalom is love, the love that God offers.

It's why God's greatest miracles don't stop when he forgives us, nor even when he rearranges our spirit, our mind and (if needed) our body.

It's why the Holy Spirit's love pours into us *and then through us to others*.

And it's why I'm pleading with you to stop and pray for a miracle even before you plunge into this book.

Because today's world tells you that staying numb is the only way to survive. *So much suffering, so many meltdowns. You can't make a difference; just focus on yourself.*

So...

Pray for a miracle... in yourself

Pray you won't stay numb *(it's a prayer we all need regularly.)*

Pray for empathy.

Pray that Jesus will show you how his miracles are healing his hurting children.

Two ways to read this book

You see, there are two completely different ways to read this book. Will it be:

a form of Christian entertainment, offering an exciting window into a world that has nothing to do with you?

Or...

an adventure into a world of compassion for others, where we sit with those who are suffering. And when God asks, "Whom shall I send? And who will go for us?" we'll reply, "Here am I. Send me."[2]

As the disciples journeyed with Jesus, they learnt what amazing miracles he could do. It took them longer, though, to see that these miracles revealed the depth of God's love. As we learn to see miracles, we'll learn above all to see God's love for those who are hurting.

Then listen for God's call. What will you reply?

"Here am I. Send me."

References

1. Colossians 1:17

2. Isaiah 6:8v

PART 1
THE JOURNEY

1: God's ways don't change

'Come over to Macedonia and help us,' begged the man in the Apostle Paul's vision[1]. How can Macedonia *not* be significant today? It was the entry point, the doorway for the Gospel that has upended the lives of all of us who live in Europe, the Americas, much of Africa and Australasia, plus millions elsewhere too.

As soon as the Holy Spirit gave Paul that vision, he and his team set sail across the northern Aegean Sea and made for Philippi, the provincial capital. It was an adventure, certainly for Paul and his friends: a new continent, different cultures, new dangers. But they said *Yes* to God's invitation, and event followed event with exhilarating speed. A local businesswoman and her family were converted, a slave girl was released from demon possession; there was violent opposition, God intervened via an earthquake and a thriving church was established.

Brother Jimmy

God's way of calling people to adventures and miracles that will impact the world has never changed. Brother Jimmy, my main contact in North Macedonia, is one of these people.

Jimmy, a Nigerian, was the third of seven children brought up as Christians to read the Bible and pray every day. At boarding school, he started questioning the existence of God. Then one night he awoke and had a heavenly vision from God which he could make no sense of. Shortly afterwards he was taken seriously ill. The local doctors could not diagnose it, and just told him that he would die quickly. In his own words...

"My mother was intense in prayers for me. The Lord gave her a vision

which she interpreted to mean that the Lord was going to show mercy to me and I would not die but live and then declare His goodness on earth. I did recover but I deliberately started to forget the Lord, and tried to run away from him.

"I fled to Macedonia and started a restaurant business that went downhill very quickly. As a broken man, I decided to rededicate my life to God again. When I was back visiting Nigeria, I joined a tiny church that fasted and prayed, almost like fanatics. It was here, for the first time, I learned to fast and one night at about 4:30 AM, I heard a loud voice, calling 'Jimmy. Jimmy. Jimmy.' It was so loud but did not burst my ear drums. Three questions were asked. 'Do you want to prosper in life? Do you want to advance in life? Do you want to move forward in life?' This sound was so sweet to my ears, and startled by the questions, I answered Yes. Yes. Yes. The voice came again: 'Do my work. Do my work. Do my work.' I was called back to Macedonia to take the Gospel where there was none, to walk with people that nobody wants to walk with, to be a mouthpiece for those who cannot speak for themselves and to fight for the marginalised."

Jimmy returned and started planting churches, mostly in the poorer towns and villages, across the country. There are now around thirty. He leads a small team of pastors that travel hundreds of miles on potholed roads, visiting groups often squeezed into rooms or small halls, teaching, ministering, and leading worship, sometimes at three or four different churches in a single day. To travel with them can be simultaneously exhausting and exhilarating.

Back in Paul's time, sharing the gospel would often lead to riots or miracles. Even today there is that sense of being on the frontline with God, not knowing what will happen next. Since Paul's days, the region has been scarred by violence and war, by the long occupation of the Islamic Ottoman Empire, by Communism, corruption, poverty and injustice. The Jesus-centred, Holy Spirit-led church that Paul started has been lost, replaced now by a combination of Orthodoxy and Islam. The "lost church" certainly makes it exciting to work for Jesus in Macedonia today.

As you step out with the Gospel on your lips, offering to pray for people in the power of the Holy Spirit, you know you are breaking new ground. Many of the older villagers were born in the communist era when atheism was taught in schools. When you are set up to do evangelism in a village and a local Christian leader tells you to his knowledge that there has not been outreach there before, you get a sense of that same pioneering experience that Paul had. You're walking on the same land that he walked. In many places you go, you are the missionary, the first to preach the Good News of Jesus to them in their lifetime.

"I am confident of this," says Paul to those first Christians in Macedonia, "that God who began a good work in you will carry it on to completion until the day of Christ Jesus" [2]. That's a pretty clear promise that God is still passionate about the Macedonian church today.

In at the deep end

I first met Brother Jimmy in 2016, when he'd come to the UK for a few days, including a visit to the New Wine Christian festival at Shepton Mallet in Somerset. This big Christian festival left an impression on him. All his small churches were scattered across the country and did not have the opportunity to meet together. Jimmy invited three of us who were in a prayer group to visit North Macedonia. His vision was to put on a conference and we would be the speakers. It seemed an impossible request. But we did not dismiss the idea.

A few weeks later as I prayed over a map of Macedonia, my attention was drawn to a town on the Eastern border, called Delcevo. A phrase suddenly came into my head. "Weeping stays for the night, but joy comes in the morning." Then I got a sense of sadness and pain pervading the people there. We prayed into whatever pain the town was experiencing and asked for the joy of the Lord to visit them. A few days later, I woke up in the middle of the night with that phrase ringing over and over in my head. I discovered it was from the Psalms.[3] I also got a sense that one day I would be sharing that message in that very town. It seemed most unlikely, and a distant possibility at best. I had never spoken abroad, and had no concept of how I might end up in Delcevo.

Incredibly, within only four weeks, I crossed the border from Bulgaria into North Macedonia for the first time on a spontaneous short break holiday with my youngest son. Everything seemed alien. I had just endured an hour of questions and demands for endless paperwork, by the border guards who only spoke Bulgarian. The small border town I crossed into, en route to our holiday destination, was none other than Delcevo.

The streets were bustling. We might have been in Greece or Turkey, but this had the feel of a place more starved of investment. It was Sunday, and the small church was scheduled to start at 1pm, just a few minutes after we arrived. Feeling relieved to have made it, we drew some wicker chairs up around a circular metal table, outside a spacious glass fronted café. Almost opposite the café was a small rented room, slotted into a row of retail buildings. The Delcevo church was no bigger than a decent sized sitting room. It was sparse. Some steel chairs were tightly packed around the walls, and on the sea blue carpet stood one small table. In opposite corners were coffee making facilities and a toilet. That was it.

A few minutes later, three of Brother Jimmy's helpers, who cover the eastern churches on Sunday, arrived. They opened up with prayer and worship. They shared that on the way they had been praying that every chair in the small church room would be full. In other words, they'd prayed for doubling of the congregation's normal size. As they looked around every seat was taken. Then three more people arrived.

Immediately I was thrown in, right at the deep end. I was handed the floor and told I should lead the church for the next 45 minutes. In a country and culture I had never experienced. Through Magdalena, my young interpreter, I started by sharing the words that I had received for Delcevo a month earlier. 'Though there is pain in the night, joy comes in the morning.' This 'pain' included the loss of many of their young and educated people to other countries. We prayed the joy of the Lord into their lives, their church and their town. The talk and translation followed on and lasted exactly the allotted time without me padding or cutting short the talk. Everyone seemed very encouraged. I was left astounded by God's provision and timing, astounded to be used in this way, for the first time, in a foreign country. I would not have thought it possible.

Take up your cross

It was right after the service that I realised the courage and sacrifice that God had called these people to. Jesus' challenge is the same today as it has always been, but so is his power.

We went back with the church leader and his family, who cooked up some traditional Macedonian food for us, which was most welcome as we had not eaten for seven hours. During this time, we learnt more of the pain that hovered like a cloud over Delcevo. Our host family had certainly not been exempt: since joining the evangelical church plant, they had faced persecution for leaving the Orthodox Church. The leader's wife had been forced out of her well-paid job, and he had been demoted to a more menial job, well below the level of his qualifications or experience. But they assured us that having Jesus in their lives more than made up for any loss. What the Apostle Paul had found in that first Macedonian church was just as true today, because the Holy Spirit is just as real, just as powerful, just as present today.

The number of evangelical Christians in North Macedonia is very small, a few thousand people only, somewhere between 0.2% and 1% of the two million population. This includes the Baptists, Methodists, and other Bible-studying, Jesus-loving Christians such as Brother Jimmy's network of churches. However, this number fluctuates a lot; its biggest challenge is not persecution but migration. One of the poorest countries in Europe, North Macedonia has an average income of about 350 Euros a month. It has a GDP less than that of the small island of Malta. 60% live below the poverty line, some unable to get enough fuel to see them through the bitter winters. There are few good jobs, so many educated people look to migrate for work and families follow.

A big church in North Macedonia would be 30 people or more. Some could double that for a short period, but then two years later could be down to just a handful. The believers have not lost faith but en masse have escaped their poverty for Germany, USA, Canada, or anywhere else with better paid work. This certainly focusses the mind of the faithful church: intense outreach and evangelism is needed just to keep the churches going.

It wasn't too challenging to visit North Macedonia on a short holiday and visit a church. But what about Brother Jimmy's invitation for three of us to help organise a national Christian Conference of worship, teaching and healing?

More than that, he was asking us to be the main speakers.

In a country that felt so different to ours, where the needs were beyond anything I'd imagined.

Where opposition (sometimes violent) was normal.

Where poverty could be extreme.

Where witchcraft and demonic activity were just below the surface.

Here, fine words would never be enough. If we couldn't rely on the Holy Spirit's miraculous work, we would be mad to take up the challenge.

Yet God had prepared us. Each of us who went out to North Macedonia for the first Easter Conference has a different back story, a tale of God at work. Before we go any further, I had better tell you mine.

Learning keys

God calls us to go on an adventure of faith.

You may get thoughts of God calling you to something which seem impossible but don't dismiss them too quickly. Be open to him finding a way for it to happen.

Sometimes there is a cost to making the decision to follow God's voice, but it is the right thing to do whatever the price.

References

1. Acts 16:9

2. Philippians 1:6

3. Psalms 30:5

2: A First Miracle, A Second Life, A Third Chance...

1959. Albert is a young man who has been brought up in a children's home in Cheddar, Somerset. He and his young wife Grace move into a council house and find the bath full of coal. The local council had deemed their caravan too damp and cold in the winter for the baby girl they were shortly expecting. The following year, Susan's brother Kevin is also born in their bedroom in Annaly Road.

1971. With Christmas and Boxing Day done, Albert, an accomplished carpenter and builder, had been decorating the children's bedroom earlier that day. Now, paint fumes linger where they are sleeping. In the early hours the boy (who had been suffering with Asthma for 7 years) is now in serious trouble. His already narrowed airways are further inflamed by the irritant and they close up completely. He awakes suddenly, not able to breathe. The boy gets up and sits on the bed. He tries to cry for help, but is too weak. He collapses on his face, and uses his last ounce of energy to bang his fist on the linoleum floor. He falls unconscious. The bang is heard in his parents' bedroom. There's no phone in the house so Albert is soon running right across the village in his pyjamas to get to the Doctor's house. Later an ambulance, from another town ten miles away, arrives outside their council house. Kevin suddenly wakes up, his breathing inexplicably back to normal. He's feeling good. In fact, his breathing has not felt so good in a long time. Expecting the worst, paramedics rush in with oxygen tanks, and are surprised to see him sitting up. They take him to Bristol Children's Hospital and keep him in for five days.

A first miracle

Whether I had clinically died or not that winter's evening, I will never know for sure. I had no recollection of a 'heaven experience' or a light at the end of a tunnel. Yet how could I have survived without breathing for so long, and with no brain damage? How did my airwaves clear so fully with no medical help? The only explanation to me was the supernatural. Growing up, I became convinced that God had done a miracle in my life that evening.

A second life

From then on, I thought of every year after the age of 11, as my second life. God had certainly given me a second chance that night. And after that he repeatedly refused to give up on me, despite my own efforts to mess things up.

I already knew *of* God. I was used to kneeling on the floor every night as a child and saying repetitive prayers of blessing for my family. "God bless Mummy and Daddy, Gran and Grandad, Aunty Valerie and Susan. Amen". Then if things were wrong in my life I would turn to God and ask for help. Desperate prayers like, "My pet tortoise has escaped, please bring him back." He was always found and brought back to me, so I knew God answered prayer.

I had no doubt that my Mum had prayed for me that night when my breathing stopped, and her prayers were answered too. Deep down I wanted somehow to honour God with my 'second life'. I had been brought up in a Baptist church with a lively Sunday school. They were big into knowing your Bible and memorizing facts, such as reciting all the book titles in the Old Testament and New Testament. This laid a foundation I would build on much later.

Two years before I had collapsed in my room, I had attended a tent ministry for children in the field directly behind my house. Perhaps there were 100 children there every day. Most of us were poor, and they gave out good prizes for well-behaved attendance. So I went a lot. As a young boy, I felt convicted of the wrong things I did, and definitely did not want to risk going to the Hell they openly spoke of. I decided I would follow Jesus. I would be a Christian. Heaven seemed a much brighter prospect to me, even if it meant having to try harder to behave myself.

Behaviour: not great!

Behaving, particularly if I was trying to do it in my own strength, would prove quite difficult, especially when I started my grammar school at 12. I was determined to be popular and worked out my own formula. It involved being really helpful to other students, selling my lunch pack, and playing the teachers up. It worked. Of course, it also meant I would sometimes be sent out of class, or I would find myself standing in front of the headmaster, or being tortured by games teachers. Once I had to write out a thousand lines. That is a lot of writing!

Though it seemed a little at odds with my behaviour, I still saw myself as a Christian and sometimes attended the small Christian Union at the school. During this time, I went to an event at the nearby Banwell Methodist church and was intrigued to hear people speaking in tongues. My Irish minister in Cheddar had taught that all such gifts of the Spirit finished with the book of Acts, never to be seen again.

Then the sixth form prefect who ran the Christian Union invited me to an event in Bristol. It was a wonderful night of worship and teaching which finished with an appeal to come forward if you wanted to be healed of something. The speaker even mentioned asthma. Part of me wanted to go forward, but it was as if I was super-glued to my seat. The opportunity passed but lived on long in my memory. If I ever got the opportunity again, I would go forward.

I did get another opportunity. I did go forward and even threw away the inhaler I was carrying.

I wasn't healed.

One Friday I turned eighteen, and on the Saturday I went out for a drinking session with my friends. We were making a noise in the High Street when a large lady from the Church, whom we sarcastically called Twiggy, accosted me. In a stern voice, she pointed out that I was being baptised the next day, and this wasn't the type of spirit I should be entertaining.

She was right, but a few months later, after my girlfriend ditched me, I downed a decent quantity of alcohol from Dad's drinks cabinet, got on my KTM unrestricted moped, and ramped it round the village as fast as I could. I came home and wept. It was not long before my A level exams and I could no longer concentrate. I did poorly in them.

The summer holidays followed on and I went on a cheap camping holiday in France. My friend and I soon ran out of beer money and took a small job sweeping down the large tents of pine needles, to earn enough to get through our fortnight. I was not in a great place with God.

A third chance

When I got back from the South of France, the results letter was waiting for me, with the news I was going to Aston University, in the centre of Birmingham. This was definitely not my first choice or what I'd hoped for. I didn't appeal. It was still a university and none of my extended family had ever been to one. In addition, I had managed to get university sponsorship with an engineering company based in Cheltenham, so I just went with it. I did not realise what a big hand God had played in this. I never regretted it.

Because I hadn't been expecting to go to Birmingham, I struggled to find accommodation at such short notice. But my Baptist minister in Cheddar knew someone who knew someone. A lad at the university's Christian Union heard of a man at Sutton Coldfield Baptist that had a spare room. It was the only thing on the table, so I took it.

At that point I had no intention of going to the Christian Union but felt obliged to go just the once to say a thank you. I could at least tell my Baptist minister that, "I tried it, but did not fit in." When I arrived, I was made to feel so welcome there that I really enjoyed the evening. I liked it so much, I went most weeks throughout my four year course. There was nothing miraculous about the meetings and I was shy and uncomfortable when we split into groups to pray. A lot of the group seemed to have a much stronger faith than I did, and they encouraged me. The quality of Christian speakers they got hold of, sometimes booked two years in advance, was top drawer. I learnt a lot and spent a fortune on a huge single volume Matthew Henry commentary, originally written in 1706, to help me study the Bible. I started writing articles for the Cheddar Baptist magazine, and people there were questioning if the writing was really mine.

"If you want to keep me, do something."

I was changing for the better, but the pull between the truth of Jesus and the world I lived in carried on relentlessly inside of me, intensifying during these college years. I was like the handkerchief tied in the middle of a tug-of-war rope.

My student apprenticeship in Cheltenham was served out with a dozen other lads. We had a strong social life that involved night clubs, drinking, swearing, and eating fried chips up to four times a day. During each of these industrial placement periods, my behaviour worsened and my faith dropped off, only to be revitalised on my return to university. I realised that, away from the Christian Union, my faith was not strong enough to keep me close to Jesus.

One evening during my final term, I knelt down in my tiny student bedroom and prayed a blunt and shockingly honest prayer. *"Lord Jesus, my next industrial period is not six months, it is forty years. If you do not do something special in my life, I will fall away from faith and you will lose me. If you want to keep me, you need to do something about it."*

After that prayer an old lady, Helen Roseveare, turned up to speak at the Christian Union. She had spent twenty years as a missionary in the Congo during violent times there, and had even been raped by the soldiers. She was tough and had great stories. Then she turned on us, especially the lads. *Why aren't you going out on the mission field? Why are you leaving this vital work for old women to do?* It was a question that stuck in my mind and would not leave. I had an answer though. There was not a missionary group anywhere that would be mad enough to take me even for a short term. I had nothing to offer.

If I was to be free of this challenge, though, I had to level this with God, so I prayed again. *Lord, if you want me to go and do a mission, I will. However, it is up to you to find an organisation that will take me, and I have my final exams coming up now, so I am not going to spend any time looking myself.* An outrageous prayer, but somehow it seemed fair enough to me.

Then they turned up. World Horizons. A group, not of old ladies, but of young men and women burning with a passion for mission and doing crazy things like driving a converted Dutch army truck across the Sahara Desert. They were no less challenging than Roseveare. Anyone interested in short term mission opportunities, they said, should come on our next information weekend in Llanelli, Wales. It looked like my prayer had been answered against expectations, so down I went and quickly signed up to a month's trip to Algeria that September.

Word got around the Christian Fellowship, and one evening before one of my final exams, there was a knock on my bedroom door. Jono was another engineering student, two years younger than me, and wanted to know if the rumours about my crazy adventure were true, because he fancied going himself.

First steps into mission

And so, later that summer, I set off with sixteen others in a transit van from London down through France, Spain and into North Africa. Once on the quieter roads, Jono and I both opted whenever we could to travel outside the van, standing on the back plate and holding on tight to the roof rack or external ladder. A little dangerous, yes, but exhilarating too. We became firm friends and eventually played the role of 'best man' at each other's weddings.

There was nothing outwardly supernatural about this trip into the Sahara and the Kabyl mountains, but in a spiritual sense it was transforming for me. I still relatively lacked confidence as a Christian so I held back from speaking out whilst on the trip. But one evening we were praying about when to tackle the difficult border crossing between Morocco and Algeria where teams could be held up for many hours, even days. After praying, I got a strong feeling that we should just go for it; we should cross late that evening and not wait until the morning. I plucked up courage to share this with the leaders. They were surprised, but put it to the whole team, and the vast majority felt this was right. At midnight, we tried it, and got through in record time. It was the first time that I realised God could speak to me and use me, despite all my weaknesses and failings.

The next year I returned to the Kabyl Mountains with Jono and with a French speaking lad called Martin. We saw more of God's miraculous provision and protection for us as we travelled by foot and public transport into this mountainous home of the Berbers. Because of Islamic persecution it was too risky for the believers there to meet with us face to face, but we could prayer walk and do some helpful fact finding for the mission group. For many years

I continued to pray for the Kabyl Christians, knowing nothing of what happened to the small churches there. Thirty-five years later I discovered there had been a revival amongst the Kabyl people and the church was now strong and vibrant and no longer in hiding.

As a young engineer I followed up my two trips to the Kabyl with a third Horizons trip. The following year I led a team of students out to Tunisia. I got sunstroke when my hired motorbike broke down on the island of Djerba near the Libyan border. I was left exposed in a forty-degree heat for too long. That night I became so ill with sunstroke that I could not move, and rested the next day in a small dark bedroom, more resembling a cave. As I lay praying, I discovered I could now pray in a supernatural language. I had wanted this for years, but received the gift of tongues just lying there alone.

Learning keys

Never underestimate what God can do in your life.

It's far better to be blunt and shockingly honest with God, than to drift along paying lip service to following him.

God will meet you in any number of ways, if you'll let him. Are you ready to be challenged?

3: God Always Knows What He's Doing...

Was life straightforward over the next 30 years? No. It was at times difficult and challenging, but also rewarding. God was shaping me through my work and my family, my mistakes and successes, my illnesses and my desire for him. If you let him, the Holy Spirit will teach you to see miracles in it all.

I kept up my involvement with World Horizons after that third trip, helping out on their information weekends, but I never went out with them on mission again. Though I went on to help lead Christian youth groups, to perform in a Christian rock band, and even to become a Christian DJ, I would not take part in another overseas mission trip for thirty years.

Collapse

Like many young twenty-somethings, I thought I could burn the candle at both ends. I was helping out with youth work at my local Baptist church, and was playing guitar in their worship band. It was a small church but we were regularly getting seventy teenagers to our evenings and seeing many get baptised after our weekends away. I was rehearsing with the band or working with young people as many hours as I was doing engineering, with just one night off a week.

The music group I was in, *Voice in the Wilderness*, started writing our own material and began gigging. My wife-to-be Jenny was playing electric double bass for the band; everything was ramping up nicely. We had one concert at a local venue supporting an old rock band called the Pirates, who had charted in the 60s.

Then I collapsed on stage immediately after our performance.

For the next seven years I fought a chronic fatigue illness known as M.E. or unkindly as 'Yuppie Flu'. Yeast, sugar, and alcohol all disappeared from my diet and I kept going the best I could with my paid employment, and youth work. It was hard. I slept a lot. The illness ebbed and flowed as I inevitably did more than I should have been doing.

I did eventually overcome it.

Dwellings and alley-ways

The Holy Spirit has a way of nudging us along, long before we realise the direction he's taking. Even though I knew he had healed me as a boy, even though I knew in theory that God heals today, I didn't really expect to see him doing it around me, let alone through me. But one day God put me in a situation where he used me to do just that.

There are three council estates that are notorious for crime in my town. I went every week to the one nearest to me and hung out with the youth, doing what I could. Sometimes I even went with them to court. They called me Kev, or Rev to my face, although they referred to me on the streets simply as 'the Christian'.

That afternoon, Terry, a teenager I'd got to know, called me over to his side of the street. I didn't recognise the two teenage friends he was with. I had, though, noticed he was limping. Crossing the road, I smiled, "What's up mate?"

"I 'urt my knee, and I gotta game on Saturday. Will you pray for it?" He was a good soccer player. I paused for a bit, not reluctant, but just thinking what to do. Most people, when they ask for prayer, expect you to go away and do something magical in your closet.

"OK, but only if I can pray for it right now in front of your mates."

He smiled back. "Yeah, do it."

We were confident enough with each other, but it was still surreal, crouching down and laying hands on his knee in front of his friends. A couple of neighbours stood in a doorway watching. Free entertainment. As I prayed, his knee warmed up, and the pain subsided. "Much better, cheers Kev." He sounded a bit surprised, but not overly so. I was probably more surprised. That was it. He was gone. He played well on the Saturday.

It was the only time I was asked to pray for sickness on the streets of the estate. Yet when the opportunity arose, I went for it. Why not? If he had limped away, he would have still been grateful that I had tried.

Nagging for a healing anointing

I had always been cautious about using the 'R' word as I felt it had become much overused at Christian gatherings. Yet I had read a lot about 'revivals' throughout recent history, particularly those in the US and the UK. I followed reports of the Toronto blessing in 1994 as it spread outwards, even touching a Congregational youth group, that my wife and I ran for 10 years, with kids falling over in the Spirit. So I was already open to such possibilities when I met Pastor Clyde from Cwmbran Victory Outreach Church in 2013, after his Christian rehab inmates had taken our church service. He asked me if I had heard what had happened at his own church. I hadn't.

53 year-old businessman Paul had been in his wheelchair for ten years after contracting osteoarthritis. He had been going to the Victory warehouse church run by these young men who had successfully passed through their Christian rehab centre. They had won their battle over addictions through praying in tongues, and

had then trained as pastors. This group included Pastor Richard who had formerly been jailed for drug offences. When Paul was prayed for by Richard at the midweek meeting, he felt a bolt of energy go down his spine and through his legs which suddenly strengthened. He jumped out of the wheelchair and held the very heavy contraption above his head like a trophy. His wife started screaming with joy. One of his legs had also been 2 and a half inches shorter, following a car accident. That had grown back too. This remarkable and unexpected healing was the catalyst for an outpouring of healing miracles in the Victory Outreach church. It became known about across the world and people flocked there. A revival of healing. They were now holding healing meetings most nights. Clyde invited us down. It was a 90-minute drive each way, but we were keen to find out more.

My friend Jason and I arrived very excited for our first time and queued to get into this large warehouse space on the edge of town. The smart foyer, equipped with a modern coffee bar, was crammed full with people wanting to get into the large, worship space beyond. A few minutes later, the black curtain dividers were opened. The worship area soon filled to capacity, leaving some still clustered outside of the building, in the drizzle, unable to get in.

As soon as we entered, the atmosphere felt thick with the presence of God. The worship and preaching were great, but the testimonies of healings, verified with medical proof, were astonishing. After this first taste, we knew we needed more. There was something palpable that we were missing and needed in our Christian lives; we felt we would find it there.

We kept returning as often as practicable. Jason and I wanted what the Pastors had, to be able to pray in the power of the Holy Spirit and see people healed. Some were being transformed during the worship time without even being prayed for. One evening a young lady, a reformed prostitute, shared from the stage that she had felt a burning sensation on her leg during the worship time. She went to the toilets to check it out and found that a tattoo, now highly inappropriate to her reformed life, had completely disappeared from her leg. Pastor Clyde joked that his friend had *just paid £200 to have a tattoo removed* and that *he should have gone to Jesus.*

By the time I heard of the meetings and started going, they were down from daily to twice a week, but I went as often as I could despite the cost, and took as many as I could with me. There were miraculous healings in every service, with medical proof of deliverances from cancer, paralysis, addictions, hepatitis, etc. Some were healed gently, some cried out loudly and bodies convulsed as their spiritual chains were broken off. There was an overwhelming atmosphere of joy, faith and expectancy. The experience ignited latent faith throughout the packed warehouse church meetings.

I wanted to run services like this, I wanted it so much. I hate seeing people sick. I do not think that it is generally God's will for someone to be miserably sick, to be in constant pain, to be fearful or depressed, or addicted. Many times, I returned to Victory Church and knelt at the front during ministry times, begging Jesus for this gift. After the services we kept nagging the pastors to pray that their anointing would also pass on to us. We were so hungry for more of God. I tapped into that for several months until the outpouring had passed and these regular services stopped.

Our own minister had also been impacted by her visits to Cwmbran and she allowed us to pray for people at the end of our own services. Dan was first; his arm was in a sling from tendonitis. Doctors had told him it was a severe case and would take a significant time to heal. As we prayed for him, I got a picture in my head of a fireball moving down within his arm from his shoulder to his hand. After prayer, he said that he felt warmth go right through his arm. Next day, he was going about his business when he realised that he had not put his sling on that morning and his tendonitis had gone. He rang us. We were amazed and excited.

Others followed, though it was by no means a regular occurrence.

One lady soldier visited the church. She had bad back pains due to a bullet lodged in her that was so close to her spine it could not be removed. We prayed for her after the service and her pain went. Later we got a message from her that she had another X-ray done, and the bullet had actually moved. The surgeons were then able to take it out.

What we had prayed so much for, had begun.

Start local

Interestingly, when Jesus sends out his disciples to tell others about the good news of God's kingdom and to heal the sick, he initially tells them just to go to the 'lost sheep of Israel', their fellow Jews that had lost their way with God. *Do not go into Samaria or other non-Jewish territories,* Jesus instructed. *Start local.*[1]

When you hear stories of miracles abroad, it is easy to discount seeing miracles in your own place, just where you are, in your everyday living. Will Jesus do the same here with me, the same as he would if I was in Macedonia or Africa? No, probably not the same, as all cultures are different, and the spiritual atmospheres over countries vary a lot. But he is definitely able to do miracles where you are. He is God after all.

Where we start from is definitely our home town, with our friends and families, and with those strangers that God allows to drift through our life from different directions:

You visit your in-laws. One of them is sick with a fever. "Can I pray for you?"

You are having a house extension done, and your builder whom you know well, is limping. "Would you like me to say a prayer for that knee?"

You see someone you vaguely know crying on a park bench. You go over and enquire. They have not slept since their partner died and they are really afraid about the future. "I believe in the power of prayer. Will you let me pray for you, that God will break that fear off you and give you his peace?"

For many people in the workplace, or in some neighbourhoods, you may be the only one who is openly a Christian. Even if there are other Christians around, you might be the only one who is confident enough to pray for the power of the Holy Spirit to change someone's life. In those situations, you are 'the Christian' – like me on the Estate. If you don't act, who will?

The local Jesus

Jesus seemed to be healing people wherever he went. Nowhere was off limits. He healed on the roadside, in villages and towns, in outdoor meeting places and in people's homes. His Father in heaven gave Jesus opportunities for demonstrating Kingdom life, with love and compassion. He saw them and took them.

Jesus is our role-model, so the world is our oyster: we can take the saving and healing love of Jesus wherever we go, and to whomever we meet. The example he gives, though, is to start in your own neighbourhood and workplaces. Start wherever you already are.

I had started local. However, just like the early disciples, my experience did not end there. Though I didn't understand it at the time, the Holy Spirit was already lining me up for the challenges of a country I knew nothing of, North Macedonia.

God always knows what he's doing.

Learning keys

Fervently ask God to give you a new spiritual gift. As Paul says to the church in Corinth, it's good to do it, *provided* that your motive is love.[2]

Get alongside other Christians whom you trust who are practising spiritual gifts.

A true revival leaves a lasting impact on society. In each one, it seems that God does something different, something new, often unsettling, even controversial in the eyes of traditionalists. Who knows when it may happen again, but if you hear of a revival happening (as it did at Cwmbran), then try to get there if you can. It will help grow your faith.

References

1. Matthew 10:5-8. Note: Later, they were commissioned by a resurrected Jesus to go and make disciples of all nations (Matthew 28:19).

2. 1 Corinthians 14:1. Note: Paul goes on to encourage the gift of prophecy, but what he writes clearly applies to all gifts.

4: Success To Everyone Who Believes?

Well, that's enough about my back story. God works miraculously in each one of his children, but sometimes we need to ask his help to see the miracles he's doing. We also need to ask him to open our eyes to his reasons for doing them. He knows what he's doing, and remember, he always wants to do much more, if we'll let him.

The Holy Spirit had certainly been working in each of the group he was calling to North Macedonia in 2016. At the start the group comprised Richard (known as Jobbo) who had first heard God's call to Macedonia, along with Jason (who had been with me at Cwmbran "nagging God" for a healing ministry) and me.

After I returned with my son from that first exhilarating visit to North Macedonia, this small group of friends started praying all the more fervently for the country and its people. We had called our prayer group the Boiler House because we meant business with God. Others in time joined us including Ian and Sue, Mario, Sinead, Ellie, Stephen and Eva. We committed ourselves to praying for the country.

Previously, all Macedonian towns had been just random names on the map that we'd bought. At one Boiler House meeting, we specifically asked God to give us some words for different towns. Each verse was written out and stuck on the map. We kept on being drawn to one town in the centre of the country: Veles. Jason got the scripture from Isaiah 61 which includes the words, "He has anointed me to bring good news to the poor". Alarmingly, as he prayed he also started getting disturbing images in his head of deformed children.

We stopped praying and Google-searched Veles, to discover that it was described as the most polluted city in Europe. This was due to soil and ground water pollution from the Topilnica smelting factory just outside the town, with high level of lead, zinc, cadmium and arsenic. Crops grown in this environment were eaten locally and caused many health problems. These included serious birth defects, such as damaged and missing organs in babies. We went back to the map and prayed for healing over the town, its people and its land.

The months ticked by. That Easter conference, daunting in its size and potential, was getting closer. We needed a team including a worship leader, we needed a big venue, and we needed to raise about £5000 in finance. Despite many hours' searching, the right venue couldn't be found. With just a few weeks to go, things were looking dire. Yet we knew this was God's idea, and we had to keep listening and trusting. We would work like it depended on us, and pray like it depended on God. We would just see what would happen. In faith, we came up with a name for the conference: 'New Hope'.

It was a Monday prayer time on 16th January 2017. That week, with just 13 weeks to go, I wrote this in the journal as a marker:

Venue, none; Worship leaders, none; Finance, none; Helpers, one; Publicity, none. We trust in him to provide. There is no chain his love can't break.

The Master Recruiter – and the clay pot

"At least I can raise some money as we're waiting," I told myself, though to be honest it was more in my own strength than in response to God's leading.

My best man Jonathan (Jono) Cox had moved to Aberystwyth in Wales; he was developing hydro projects there and his wife

Heather was now a doctor in general practice. At Christmas, I had shared with Jono that I was thinking of getting a small number of individuals or churches to sponsor £500 each. Most of the money we needed to raise was to cover the cost of transporting people to the event in coaches and feeding them all. Many Macedonians are unable to afford this themselves, and we wanted to give everyone in these poor churches the opportunity to attend the conference. Jono said that he would talk to his Rector at St. Mikes[1] whom he thought might be interested in getting their church to support us with prayer and finance. Sounded good.

He later rang me and invited me to go and share the vision at his church in a 10-minute Q&A session at their evening service, I was full of doubt. I was expecting an invite to preach there at least. Could I justify a six hour round trip, and a full tank of petrol for 10 minutes, when there was no guarantee of support for New Hope? It wasn't making sense to me. But God's ways are not our ways. I rang up my 'best man' with the intent of saying 'No'. His phone was still ringing when I heard God's voice in my head say, *Really Kevin, you won't do that for me?* When Jono picked up the phone, I felt different words come out of my mouth, "Yes, that's fine Jono, let's do it."

Whilst I was on the long drive to West Wales in the car, I got another word from God, which seemed quite random. *Before you do the Q&A with Jono, say that there's someone here that God wants to step out in mission work. They're worried that they can't do it. God is saying that "I want that person's availability, not ability; I'll provide that person with all that's needed."*

So I shared exactly that, then answered Jono's questions about Macedonia and myself, for just ten minutes.

After the service I joined the church prayer team. One young lady made a bee-line for me. "I was the one you were talking to," she said. "It was me."

I looked at Freya, and the words just came out of my mouth,

"And you are coming to Macedonia?" "Yes, I think I am," came the slightly stunned reply. Later I went to the back of the church, and another lady, a nurse of about my age, Brenda, came up to me and quietly said that she had heard God's voice ask her recently to do some mission work, but she didn't have the confidence to go. She had regretted that decision and had prayed, *Give me another opportunity and I will go*. The next day, I got word that another young lady from that Church called Emma, also wanted to join our team.

From what I remember of that evening, I simply appealed for prayer and finance support. Although I had encouraged involvement in mission generally, I don't remember saying anything at all about people joining our mission trip. When I got back to Jono's house after the evening service I was filled with an overwhelming sense of God's goodness and his presence came over me like a flood. Words rang in my head: "We now have this light shining in our hearts, but we ourselves are like fragile clay jars containing this great treasure. This makes it clear that our great power is from God, not from ourselves." [2] As I went to my guest bedroom there were tears in my eyes.

No doubt about it: I was the unworthy clay pot that night. I left Aberystwyth, with the financial support I had wanted, as well as prayer support and three wonderful new members for the Mission Macedonia team. If I had listened to my own voice, I would have got nothing.

Prophetic art

There were only a few weeks to go. But God was lining things up. Another three people joined up, including (crucially) Simon, a worship leader. Along with Jason's wife and their two children, aged 9 and 15, we now had a visiting team of 13.

It was a God-picked team, we soon discovered, with all the talents we needed. Unusually, there was at least one person in each of the first seven decades of life, with a wonderful mix of gender, background and talents. It proved to be a team where each person far exceeded their own expectations, including the children. They all gave fully of themselves every day, and despite living in close proximity for a week, I didn't hear a single argument. We hadn't picked the team, we had listened to Jesus, and he had picked the team. In fact, before the mission, there was no one team member that knew everybody else – well, except Jesus, of course.

What about money? He had that covered too. One Sunday, for instance, I was passed on an envelope from an anonymous gift of £250 in cash. Children at one church raised £1000 by filling Mission Macedonia jam jars with money. By the time we went, we had all the finances we needed.

But how could New Hope go ahead without a venue? Only one had been offered up to us, which was an indoor sports arena in that central town of Veles. I had a photo of the venue printed out on A4 paper. The building was so big that it looked completely impracticable.

One recent recruit to our team was Sally, whose prophetic gifts were expressed through her art work, something completely new to me. She would pray, listening to God, and then she would pen or paint what she heard. We enlisted her help.

The first painting Sally sent along to our Monday meeting was of a fisherman pulling a net of fish into his boat, with helpful scriptures written around the drawing. She had coloured in sections of the net in green, orange and yellow. It was a combination of colours she had never used before, but she felt they had strong significance.

That evening at our Boiler House prayer meeting, we were still agonising about the venue. I looked down to the table, and right next to the photo of the large indoor venue was Sally's artwork. The colours of the sports arena pitch matched the colours in the net even down to the shade. The penny dropped. The sports arena in Veles would be God's net where we'd catch his fish. That was where people would be saved.

At Easter, when we finally walked into the stadium, hung up on the wall at the back were nets. God sees the end from the beginning.

You are not inviting me; I have invited you

Easter, though, was still a few weeks away. We had the venue, the team, the finance, but what we needed was a whole lot more faith. So we prayed. At one meeting, I started saying, 'Lord, we invite you...' I was going to come with a shopping list of things for him to engage in. I felt him stop me mid-sentence and say to me. *You are not inviting me, Kevin. I have invited you. I have invited you to come and work with me in Macedonia on what I have already started out here.*

Sure enough, one of Sally's prophetic artworks featured a bridge built between us and the Macedonian church people. Some of the words on that artwork read:

'Your going is in answer to their prayer. They asked me to send support. They need to know I heard and care. Go and build them up. I will make a way where there was no way. God is paving the way, and the way is reinforced with his blessing, his words, his plan. Every piece will come together, trust him. Follow my lead one step at a time. Come and see what I have already begun. Go and build them up. Bring what you have and watch what God's rich anointing can do with it and through you'.

Success to everyone who believes?

Did we expect the Holy Spirit to work, or did we not? That was what it came down to. A few days later Brother Jimmy sent us the conference publicity he had prepared. It was a shock to see what he had put on the flyers for the event. And the same message was going out for two weeks on local TV and radio in Macedonia.

New Hope. – a week of Godly healing. You have been to your Doctor recently and you have received a scary diagnosis, or you have been sick for a long time without any improvement. Maybe you are not sick but you still feel that there is something that is not right in your life, or in theory you should be successful, but actually things are really bad, or your family relationships are a real battlefield. Jesus is the cure. His servants Jobbo, Kevin and Jason who are guests in Macedonia, are inviting everyone who wants a cure and solution. These guests from England will bring success to everyone who believes.

We were astonished to read this. Could he really be talking about us? This is a level of expectation far beyond anything we had imagined. At first, we were agitated by it. But then tried to relax and trust Jimmy in this. Much more important, we trusted God, a bit, anyway. We would fail spectacularly or succeed spectacularly. At that stage, we had no idea which it would be.

So... more prayer. During our Monday night prayer sessions before the trip, we prayed for words about healing. *Jesus, whom do you intend to heal when we're there? Just give us a clue. What can we call out for healing?* In listening to God, the first words I received on this were very clear and specific. A thought kept repeating itself in my head, with no other thoughts crowding it out. *There will be a lady with complete deafness in her left ear.* I wrote that down. That was the first of several specific words.

Doubt came flooding back and fighting it was difficult. In Jason's house, in our prayer meeting we could hear things and write things down, even look at encouraging pictures, but would God actually turn up in power? Would we really see Macedonian people come and get saved in this sports arena? Would we really see any one restored to health at all, let alone a deaf ear completely healed? It seemed a world away from what we had known to date.

Learning keys

Listen, trust and obey.

Remember that God wants your *availability*. Don't see your ability as the answer or your lack of ability as the problem; when he calls, God will provide all that's needed.

References

1. St Michael's Church, Aberystwyth

2. 2 Corinthians 4:7

5: Prayer: Expect The Unexpected

"Now faith is confidence in what we hope for and assurance about what we do not see."[1]

In other words, if you're going to pray that God will work miracles in your church, your family, your street, you have to start expecting the unexpected.

In Easter 2017, we all felt we were flying into the unknown, the unexpected.

Flights into Macedonia had proven too expensive at Easter for us, so we opted for the cheaper option of flying to Sofia in Bulgaria, where two minibus vans arrived from Jimmy to pick us up and drive us across the border and into the heart of Macedonia.

No-one really knew what to expect, but spirits were high. Everyone was excited and taking in the new and changing landscapes. Mountains rose up, rivers raced then meandered. Vineyards led into villages of flat-topped concrete homes, mostly solar-powered and unfinished. Traffic slowed behind the tractors and horse-drawn carts.

Three Taps

We had set off from Cheltenham at 2 a.m. Twenty hours later, as the evening drew in, we came off the highway onto an unmade road which looped past an Orthodox church, open twice a year, and drove alongside a closed convenience store. We had arrived at Tri Chesmi (Three Taps). Turning into a residential road, we drew up outside a pair of semi-detached houses, with both dwellings being used by the mission. The front doors were reinforced by locked metal grills.

Inside was an Aladdin's cave of outreach material, piles of evangelistic hand-outs, clothes for the poor, musical instruments and, at the foot of the stairs, a large pair of shiny gold shoes, Jimmy's. A Macedonian teenage girl, Selvinas, was assigned as our housekeeper for the week, and we were under strict instructions to let her serve us, and not try do the British thing and make teas or coffees ourselves regardless. We had our assignment to serve and she had hers.

We slept, then got acclimatised to our new surroundings when we woke on Good Friday. Our first task was to take a service in the patio area in front of the mission house for the local villagers. A vine-dressed pergola provided some shelter. We shared some thoughts and scriptures and had our first attempt at singing a chorus in two languages. We asked if anyone wanted healing prayer. Only one lady responded. She had pains in her head, knees and spine. We worked together, praying for her. Progress was slow but we persisted in prayer. Bit by bit the pain in the different areas of her body all went. She was delighted. We were delighted. This was our first miraculous healing in Macedonia, and it set a pattern for all our trips from then on. We would now allow time after a service to pray for Holy Spirit's power to come on anyone, whatever the need, and then see what Jesus wanted to do.

After seeing this first lady healed, everyone else at the meeting asked for prayer. That day we prayed against bronchitis, numb hands, lumbago, an abusive husband, insomnia and sinus problems. As far as we could tell, each person was touched by God through the prayers. Whilst some healings were instant, in other cases we could not know or test what would happen, so had to trust God for the answers. The team was beginning to listen more to God's promptings, supporting each other with insights into different conditions. Nurse Brenda tended to understand what the symptoms meant; this, coupled with spiritual insight, helped target our prayers more accurately at the root cause.

Into the centre

Veles was real after all, not just a name on the map. On our second day we were driven to the central town where Jimmy's team had a long term rental on a single room for their church. Whilst praying in the Boiler House, one thing that we felt strongly directed towards was to have a day to encourage and teach the youth and young leaders. Jimmy had arranged this and we crammed into the room for our worship, prayer and teaching. It was the first time we experienced songs being sung simultaneously in different languages, and it created a beautiful atmosphere. We led a practical session on healing ministry, where they rehearsed how to do it on each other. When one of the older regional leaders was healed of her pain, it set everyone off in the right direction. Looking back, I am amazed by how confident we were to teach others when we had so little experience ourselves.

After being packed like sardines into the Veles church we were about to go to the other extreme. God's great fishing net had been prepared.

Gemidgii

The concrete stadium was a formidable example of the brutalist architecture from the communist era. It is named after a revolutionary group who had used terrorist acts to draw attention to the Ottoman oppression of Macedonia, hoping to change international public opinion. We were not terrorists ourselves but we did want to see change, a Jesus revolution which ousted the evil spiritual forces from *their* oppression of Macedonia.

Jimmy's team had erected a huge sign. It re-iterated their expectations.

Today Jesus continues to perform Miracles, gives sight to the blind, heals the sick and brings good news to the poor.

The verse[2] we had stuck over Veles on the map was reflected well in this pronouncement. We had come indeed to bring good news to the poor, and in announcing release to the captives. We also hoped to see the blind and the sick restored. Break every chain, Lord.

The stadium was hired for two days. We were expecting a few hundred people for New Hope, but the venue was large and could seat 4000. It looked as if it had been a long time since the last event. Everything was very dusty. There was a lot of work to be done inside to make it work for the conference the next day.

Jimmy had assembled a sizable, hardworking team to do just that. They cleaned down the surface of all the seats in the bleachers which rose up high at the stadium's rear. A couple of hundred more chairs had been put immediately in front of the bleachers; the microphones and PA were set up on the 5-a-side pitch facing the chairs. Just one half of the whole stadium was used. Toilets and floors were cleaned, and points set up for giving out water and merchandise.

Once the hard work was done, we held the Easter Sunday service for those churches close enough to join us, and had our time of healing afterwards. This was only our third day but we were already getting used to seeing people healed. One large man had problems with his ears that amongst other things had been giving him loss of balance, but it was intermittent. I prayed for him but he was unsure straight away if he had been healed or not. The next day I saw him again, stewarding in the car park. I asked him how his ears were now, and he threw his arms in the air and shouted, "Wonderful." In the years that followed, whenever I saw the same man again in Veles, he would tell me how well his ears were.

We were all ready to have our New Hope conference on Easter Monday. At least, we thought we were. Jobbo, Jason, and I had each prepared separate talks for New Hope, and we each had very different styles of delivering a message. Jimmy had a late surprise for us. He decided that he wanted just one message from us. He wanted us to do it together, tag preaching. The concept is that you speak in turns and tag each other in and out. We all looked shocked and were initially silent for a while. Then I asked him if he had actually seen anyone do this before. No, he hadn't – though he had once heard that twin girls had done it. *What?*

One thing was certain, and that was the three of us did not have the similar thought patterns that twins might possess. Somewhat reluctantly, we agreed to be taken even further outside of our comfort zone and give it a go. Doing this in front of potentially hundreds of people was daunting. None of us had spoken to so many people before, let alone tag-preached whilst using translators.

Nerves and excitement

Sleep was hard to find that night. I was up by 5 a.m., praying and writing down words of encouragement from God. One scripture resonated in my head, '*My power is made perfect in weakness*'.[3]

After half an hour of praying, I suddenly felt broken with a huge feeling of inadequacy and unworthiness. What right did I have to be representing Jesus at such a big occasion for the Macedonian Church? God encouraged me with words planted firmly into my mind.

Get up, be bold, stand in my truth, lift your head up and see my hand at work.

We were all up and about for an early team meeting. There was nervousness combined with excitement. This was it. A flood of promises came through as we listened to God that morning. In my notebook I scrawled down what I had heard.

'For each of us, this is the most significant spiritual day of our lives so far. Listen to faint impressions and go for it, if you are wrong you are wrong but go for it anyway. I have more than you can take, but take as much as you can. Keep your head looking up and be filled with joy, for your joy will be your strength.

We took our two minibuses to Veles, and prayer-walked the building, as the coaches arrived from all over Macedonia. Stewards were on duty; meet and greet in place; free water ready to be distributed; and the worship group were practicing. It really felt like a proper conference. New Hope was born in Veles, Easter 2017.

Then they came and they kept coming, about 500 visitors, many of whom were not yet Christians. They had presumably come primarily to experience or witness the healings, or perhaps just for a good day out.

The excitement at the event was palpable. One of the team said she had seen into the spirit world, and there were angels circling the stadium.

The birth of New Hope

Jimmy welcomed all the different churches one by one, made them stand up and prayed a blessing over each. We had a half hour of worship then one of the younger adults kicked off with an incredibly sad life story of rejection, abuse, and depression. She followed up on how she had met Jesus and was transformed by him. People were riveted by her testimony. You could see on their faces the impact it was having on them as they identified with her pain.

Then the smallest Macedonian children there led the prayers, before we went into our time of preaching.

The two passages we had been given months ago for Veles and Delchevo became key passages in our preaching that day. I kicked it off with 15 minutes on the Easter story from Gethsemane to the Resurrection, weaving in the phrase 'though there is pain in the night, joy comes in the morning'[4]. Jobbo took the baton: *Jesus is alive today, he wants to give you life today.* Jason fed off us both with lively gospel pictures and testimony. The three of us tag preached with translators for 80 minutes.

For that whole period, I felt electrified with the power of God around me and in me. I kept my head up and listened for the inner promptings of when to step forward and take the microphone and when to stop. I had never felt so alive.

When we finished, Jimmy stepped forward and gave an appeal for anyone who wanted to respond by accepting Jesus into their lives for the first time. Who wanted to have their life transformed by Jesus today? My Dictaphone was left on, and captured me saying, *"Wow. Look at that!"* as fifty or more stood up in response, including a significant number of big Macedonian men and teenage boys. It was indeed good news to the poor.

Angels with brooms

Then Jimmy turned to me and said, "Ministry now: what do you want to call out first?" I thought back to our Boiler House prayer times and told Jimmy to call out ears, anybody with hearing problems or ear pains.

More than a dozen people came forward and lined up shoulder to shoulder, facing us at the front. The other team members joined Jason, Jobbo and me. We were split up and given a translator each. I took a deep breath, and decided to go the lady furthest away on the end of the line and start there. I asked her what was wrong; the translator came back to me and told me what she had said.

"I have no hearing at all in my left ear."

It is a moment in time I often go back to. I had heard Jesus tell me in a prayer time that there would be a lady who was completely deaf in her left ear. Then the first person I pray for at the conference is that lady. The fact that I heard it in advance during a prayer meeting gave me the confidence that Jesus was going to answer the prayer. I had never seen a deaf ear healed before. Yet I had to believe it and go for it.

It is a bit like that moment when as a child you climb the steps to the highest diving board, you walk along it and look down. You have reached the point at which you either jump, which is what you came for, or you go back down the steps defeated. I jumped in. I blessed her, then commanded the ear to be healed in Jesus' name. After a few minutes of praying, I clicked my finger gently by her ear, and checked in with her. She came back to me that her hearing had been fully restored.

About the same time, Jobbo was praying for another lady who was also completely deaf in her left ear. She had come with the explanation of being born with a bone missing from her inner ear, so it was physically impossible for it to work. As he prayed, her hearing was also fully restored, and presumably the bone had been recreated inside her ear.

Jimmy kept out of the prayers but was armed with a microphone. He asked the lady with me what had happened and she confirmed her deafness had gone. Her testimony spurred others on to come forward, and so it continued.

I moved on to the next person, then the next, whilst the rest of the team were praying for others too. One small girl with a pain behind her ear had been brought forward by her mother. I knelt down and told her I would say a blessing for her and ask Jesus to take away the pain. Almost as soon as I spoke the prayer, her face was split by a huge smile. The pain had gone.

I may have prayed for up to twenty people, and only recall two where it was clearly evident that they had not been physically healed. One was a young lady with partial sight and also a young man who was profoundly deaf. On the latter, I found tears in my eyes when there was no breakthrough.

I had yet to learn how to deal properly and gracefully with those instances where Jesus doesn't heal for whatever reason. I think though that there is a cost to engaging in healing ministry. The awkwardness and pain of unanswered prayer seemed to me to be part of the cost you pay for the privilege of praying for the sick.

Some of the team had never prayed for healing on their own before, but they had no choice now, because there were so many people wanting healing. We were all caught up in the moment, trying our best to believe our eyes, process these new experiences, and learn quickly as we progressed from one person to the next. Jimmy captured all the testimonies he could on the microphone. Mario blended in with proceedings and quietly filmed everything he could. The more that were healed and testified the more that came down from their seats, and they came with every type of physical illness, addictions, tragic life situations and more.

Some people were so desperate now for prayer that they were pushing in. Some tried to thrust children at us, over the heads of others. Some of the team were physically being pushed backwards in the rush to get blessed by God. We all prayed for the best part of two hours, with a short break for communion.

It was an awesome scene that no one from the UK team nor the Macedonian team had ever expected or witnessed before.

Our finance had provided everyone with food as well as transport. It was only our team that did not eat (there was no time.) When the last person had gone, we were left exhausted but transformed. What we had heard God say in our minds, through scriptures and through each other, had come true in a most dramatic fashion.

Before the conference, Sally had drawn a very moving image of giant angels with large brooms sweeping the sports arena from the centre out to the sides. These warrior janitors were, in Sally's words, *sweeping away all the broken chains.*

We had indeed been anointed to work with God and his angels, to bring good news to the poor. As Brenda said, the key was that we had spent the last year praying together.[5] Jimmy's outlandish advertising had been accurate after all. It had been a week of Godly miracles and healing. New hope for North Macedonia.

Learning keys

If you're going to pray that God will work miracles in your church, your family, your street, you have to start expecting the unexpected.

God frequently links prophecy with healing. Listen to what the Holy Spirit is saying and follow his lead.

Some healings are instant, but others are not: you cannot know or test what will happen, so you have to trust God for the answers.

There is a cost to engaging in healing ministry. For many, the awkwardness and pain of unanswered prayer (or at least prayers that have no immediate or obvious answers) are part of the cost you pay for the privilege of praying for the sick.

References

1. Hebrews 11:1

2. Isaiah 61:1

3. 2 Corinthians 12:9

4. Psalm 30:5

5. https://youtu.be/JhaJAPU6abk (Documentary. Miracles in Macedonia)

6: The Battle Is The Lord's

Why aren't people catching the vision?

Following the drama of our first New Hope conference, I assumed the news of all the miracles we had seen would blow people away and we would be inundated with people wanting to come out on our next trip. In fact, there was a surprising amount of indifference to our testimonies. Why weren't people catching the vision?

Then we had our first major blow to the team when one of our founder members, Jason, struggling with some life issues, pulled out of prayer meetings.

Meanwhile another team member, Mario, had edited all the footage he had filmed on our trip, finally producing a professional-standard one-hour documentary called *Miracles in Macedonia*[1]. We had a launch party for the film where we tried to engage more support for the charity and for our next Easter trip out. The film gave a wonderful picture of all the miracles and our surprised responses to all that was happening. Like the talks we had given, though, it did not make the impact we expected. No one seemed particularly moved by the healing miracles, or by anything else God had been doing. We were very disappointed.

As Easter approached again, there was a big question mark hanging over it: who would actually be available to put on the next New Hope conference?

Who is pulling the plough?

Yet in the months leading up to the trip, people gave us encouraging words and prophecies about what God would do in Macedonia when we got there. One Sunday night at my home church, someone gave me the following prophecy:

"The work I have been doing will not be unfruitful (says the Lord). The seeds I have planted will bear a harvest. The Lord himself will turn over the soil for you with his hands and make the soil fruitful."

God going ahead of me, and preparing people to hear what I preached? A good harvest, with many coming to faith? Yes, but where was our team? Why was everything so difficult?

The next evening at the prayer meeting, our prophetic artist Sally gave me a picture she had already drawn for me: two strong oxen pulling a plough. I am behind the plough with my Bible, gently steering it. Over the oxen were the scripture words, 'His incomparably great power for us who believe'[2]. Sally had these words of explanation:

In this picture, God is taking the lead. It his field, and his oxen (i.e. his power) are doing the work. But he loves sharing this time with you, from ploughing, to sowing, to harvest. He can't wait to show you how he's moving. There is an ease in it. He will do the hard work.

In just two days from two different sources, I had received a strikingly similar prophecy. But where was the team?

Freya was the only person from the first New Hope that opted to come out again with Jobbo and me. She had been very popular with the Macedonians, especially the children, and had a strong prophetic ability. One other lady, Sinead, also signed up. A year ago, I thought we would be turning people away in their dozens who wanted to come on our next trip, but with a few days to go, that was it – the four of us. Critically we had no worship leader. It felt disastrous.

We were within a week of going when Freya suggested I rang Mark, a talented worship leader from her old church. I did think that the odds of him coming out for a week at almost no notice seemed ridiculously slim, but had nothing to lose in asking him. After just a day to think about it, he said yes. I was astonished. We had our worship leader, and of course he turned out to be the perfect fit.

You are a prophet

Only five of us flew out, less than half the size of last year's team. Fortunately, God isn't limited by our meagre resources (just look at Gideon's handful of soldiers.[3]) Fortunately too, the planning was in the hands of Brother Jimmy, who has a very clear view of what the Holy Spirit can do.

By the end of the first four days of our visit we had led three church services and five restaurant evangelism events. God's power was so obviously at work, saving and healing people (I kept being reminded of Sally's picture of the oxen).

But how vital it was to be aware of the spiritual war we were in. On the face of it, the town of Gostivar was a safe sort of place. It was affluent, with its casinos and shops selling gold jewellery. We were to speak in a restaurant, as we had done elsewhere. The team member who was to speak was already up front when Jimmy took the rest of us to one side. He said that a man had arrived, intending to disrupt our meeting. He had flyers to give out to discredit what we were saying about Jesus.

Not surprisingly, Jimmy wanted us to pray about how we would deal with this threatening situation. Immediately we got into a prayer scrum and listened to God.

After a few minutes, Sinead felt that it should be me that engaged with the man and prevented him from handing out the flyers. I agreed, but I needed an 'in', something prophetic that I could share about him which would grab his intention. Freya looked up and said, "He's lost someone he loved, a mother or a sister, and he blames himself." Wow! That would do it.

The man had settled down in the restaurant. I approached him and asked if I may sit with him, and he readily agreed. We exchanged some pleasantries.

"Excuse me, but may I ask you a question?"

"Of course," he replied.

"Have you recently lost someone you love, perhaps your sister or your mother?"

"Yes, yes, I lost my mother."

I looked him straight in the eyes, and with empathy I said, "And you blame yourself for it, don't you?"

He was totally disarmed by the comment. "You are a prophet!"

By the end of the meal, we were firm friends. We had photos taken together, and exchanged details and were still talking long after many had made commitments to Jesus then left. He never gave out a single flyer.

Our whirlwind tour across the country was to be followed by our two conference events. First, we met with the young leaders, gathered together from across the country in the central city of Velez. We were getting used to being crammed into the church meeting room there. We taught God's word, but also gave workshops on listening to God, on prophecy, and guidance on healing prayer. We saw the Spirit flow strongly over the young people, with some being released into prophecy and other spiritual gifts for the first time. One of the youngest girls had brought a friend whom she led to Christ during the meeting.

After this half day event, we then moved to the indoor sports arena that we had hired for the main conference. We needed to set up for the next day, and to give the mixed English and Macedonian worship group their one and only chance to rehearse.

New Hope 2018

It felt so good to be back. The Gemidgii stadium was both imposing and welcoming. Behind the rows of loose chairs, the army-green plastic seats in the bleachers rose up sharply for 18 levels, and for the first two hours the number of delegates kept growing as more coaches arrived.

If we were in a war, God was going to win. Yes, we delivered a similar mix of worship, testimony, food, preaching, and salvation call as before, but we now knew that what people wanted most from these conferences was to experience the healing power of God in prayer. Two hours at the end of the day were reserved just for prayer; everyone would get a chance to be prayed for.

But how on earth could we cope? Last year at our first conference our eleven adults had been swamped. Now there were just five of us. This year we definitely needed a new strategy: between us and the Macedonian team we would have six groups of 3 people praying. Each of us on the UK team would be assigned a translator and a young leader who had shown promise at the previous day's conference. As we prayed for healing, we would take time to teach them and help them learn on the job.

A stupid risk?

Right at the start, we would call out one person, pray for healing and get the testimony over the microphone, to show God's healing power was at work. Then we would invite everyone forward to join one of six organised queues. Was it a stupid risk? What would we do with the next 2 hours if God did not heal the first person? But we were confident; Jesus was with us, and never really doubted he would heal. We had seen him at work already.

Jimmy asked me what to call out. We had prayed many times about this in advance, and the area that came through strongest was for arthritic hands. Though we also had a strong sense that God would also be healing people with depression including those who had had suicidal thoughts.

Jimmy asked anyone with bad arthritic pains in their hands to come forward, and there were a few willing to be put on the spot. There was a confusing huddle of people around Jimmy, but one lady seemed the worst off as she had these pains in both hands and in her arms, and she also had restricted movement in them. Jimmy drew her to the front where she could be seen. Her eyes, curtained by her dark straggling hair, looked up expectantly. We laid hands on her shoulders and prayed.

It all happened so quickly. In a moment she was healed, and kept flicking her hands and fingers to show their new movement. She then gave a quick testimony to those gathered. Long queues suddenly materialised in front of us. Before we knew it, everyone's anticipation was soaring.

My young leader was almost shouting when she prayed, which I thought might be intimidating, so I tried to get her to lower her voice and soften her tone. She told me that she only had one volume. She did manage eventually.

We immediately started to see the power of God working in those we prayed with. As each stepped forward believing for their healing, they were filled with the Holy Spirit, blessed and healed. I had two depressed young men who both had suicidal thoughts, and in my mind I saw the dark cloud lift from them and the peace of God breakthrough. It transformed their facial appearance. The miracles and blessings happened in every line. Some people got saved as they were healed, some were released into tongues. It was an astonishing time where the power of God just kept coming and coming all over the stadium.

The more we gave out, the more tired we became, but eventually we had got through everyone. A traditional Macedonian band had set up and was just starting to play. In response, people were coming down from the raised seating area into the arena to dance. We were done, or so I thought.

Tumour

Just as I was going to sit down and rest, two young men approached me. One had brought his friend, whom I guess had been reluctant to come up on his own. The ill young man, probably in his early twenties, looked sad and worried. My heart sank when I looked at him as I could see that the right side of his face under his baseball cap, next to both his eye and mouth, was being pulled downwards. The skin was being stretched by something. I asked what it was, though I knew. He just said the word '*tumour*'.

I decided to move to the side of the raised seats where we could be freer from distraction and away from the arena as the music rose up in volume. Then I had a thought. I turned to my Macedonian helper and said, "You can pray as loud as you like for this one." We were emboldened by a whole series of amazing healings, so just went for it. I had my fingers lightly resting on the young man's face, and could feel the presence of God on him.

Although I tell the prayer team to keep their eyes open when they pray, on this occasion I had closed my own eyes, as I was concentrating hard on prayer. After a while, I pressed gently down on his right cheek to feel for the tumour. There was indeed something hard, but what was it? I pressed on the other check to make a comparison and realised what I was now feeling was just his cheek bones. Both sides of his face felt the same. At this point, I stood back to look at his face, and when I saw it, I didn't know what to say or believe. I was looking at his face, but my mind would not accept what I was seeing. I asked him what he felt. He kept repeating, "It feels so different, it feels so different".

I didn't say anything more, I couldn't. Instead, I took him to a gym in an adjoining room where I knew there was a large mirror. He looked at himself, tears in his eyes, overcome by what he saw. He cried, "It's gone. It's gone." We hugged each other. Then a thought came to mind that we must find Jimmy who had the microphone and get the lad to share his incredible testimony.

He agreed, but as we stepped back into the stadium, the ministry area was full of dancers in large circles going through the traditional steps. I held the lad's hand whilst I scanned for Jimmy and tried to pull him in the right direction. A lady suddenly grabbed my arm and yanked me towards her. "Kevin, you should dance." In no time, I had lost the young man, but then it didn't seem to matter anymore. Everyone was having a great time. *This has been the best Christian conference in the world – ever,* I thought to myself.

Learning keys

You are yoked to Jesus, but he will do the heavy lifting.

A prophetic word can unlock an awkward situation.

Don't be discouraged if others do not believe your testimonies. It is still right to share what God has done.

References

1. https://youtu.be/JhaJAPU6abk (Documentary. Miracles in Macedonia)

2. Ephesians 1:19

3. Judges 7

7: Onwards And Upwards

More hope

After the first two New Hope events in 2017 and 2018, we agreed that the conference should become an annual fixture. Mission Macedonia was now established as a recognised charity, fundraising to support the Macedonian churches, and we were still meeting every Monday for prayer. We were now organising smaller group trips between the main Easter ones. Every time we went out, we saw God doing miracles through our ministry. It became an expectation on our team, and we had to be vigilant to keep the focus on Jesus and give him all the glory.

My youngest son, Simeon, came out on the 2019 New Hope Conference, which was our biggest to date in terms of both team members and numbers attending. Jimmy had drawn in some other friends to help from France, Hawaii, Croatia and Pastor Angel from Bulgaria. At the main event, back in the Gemidgii stadium, we finished with our two-hour prayer ministry time. We had placed those who had less experience in healing prayer (or none at all) with the slightly more experienced. Simeon was put with Angel, whose first prayers saw a lame person get out of a wheelchair.

At the end of our marathon prayer session, I caught sight of Simeon. "Hey, lad, how did you get on?" "Well Dad, there was such a crowd pressing in on Angel that I got separated from him. I found Ian, so we teamed up. Neither of us really knew what we were doing, but people were getting healed anyway, so hey-ho." That was possibly my favourite quote from any trip. It is also a reminder that whilst you may not really know what you are doing, praying for miracles is not a leap into the dark, but is a step into the light.

Blind eyes

The global Covid pandemic ensured that New Hope 2020 did not happen. We found new ways to adapt our ministry and support of the Macedonian team, who kept open all the churches they could.

I had booked a team trip to Macedonia during 2020 despite the heavy restrictions, but in the end I was the only one able to go. Previously, I had always been out there with others, and now self-doubt re-emerged. *Would God still work through me?*

Whilst there, I had wanted to try something new; I volunteered to lead an extended service at the most northern church-plant in the mountain town of Kriva Palanka. The building was tucked down a small single-track road. It had a light airy room fronted by a gravelled garden space that was great for overspill and barbecues, and was shaded by a mature walnut tree. Sun streamed through the glass frontage, striking the green walls and bright pink cloth that lay over the front table. It was a great place to be.

Church members had invited new people along as requested. We worshipped, I spoke, and then we had an extended time of ministry. Food was provided and there was a freedom in not having to rush off to the next church. It went even better than I had hoped, the numbers there doubling, with several being saved and healed. I was delighted.

I had wanted to repeat this at Delcevo, the church on the Bulgarian border where I had first spoken way back in 2016. Yet, this time the preparation all seemed to be going wrong. On the day, only 18 came and I had prepared for nearly twice that number. These were mostly church folk too, as they had not invited their friends and families as requested. I also knew that there had been some problems with unity in the church, so I spoke on the 'Love of God', and Jesus' call to 'Love one another', and didn't do the salvation appeal. Otherwise, we went with the same format that I had used at Kriva, asking for healing in their seats, worship, testimony, the word, then food and further healing prayers.

As the service drew to a close, I felt I had failed to do what I set out to, and was fighting feelings of disappointment. But God was in the room. Again, people were blessed in their seats and miraculously healed including one man who had no feeling at all on his left foot and toes and was now happily wriggling them.

It was when I invited people forward for individual prayer at the end, that the special moment came. The first in line was Beti, who had been led to the front by a friend. How had she got there first in the rush forwards for prayer? She was slim, serene, and held herself well for a lady of 93 years. Her white hair looked groomed and she was dressed smartly. Her friend stayed by her, holding her hand and smiling.

I looked into Beti's milky eyes and asked her what she would like prayer for. She said she was blind and wanted to 'see a little'. I asked what she could already see, and she replied that it was just total darkness. Normally I would be facing down doubt over such a big prayer but there was something about the anointing in the room that seemed to plant at least a mustard seed of faith in me. I prayed for Beti, believing God would do something. I waited a little, allowing time for the Holy Spirit to move. Then she suddenly spoke.

"I can see light," Beti exclaimed to me through the interpreter. I prayed again and then astonishingly she pointed to my shirt and to the Mission Macedonia logo. "That's red," she exclaimed. She was right. Red on grey. I wondered when the last time was that she had seen a colour. Greatly encouraged now, I prayed again for more, and then she looked at me and gently said, "I can see your face." Her voice was soft now, as if she was slowly drinking in the realisation of what Jesus was doing for her. Then without warning, she quickly turned away, and disappeared out of the door with her friend. I didn't even know how much of her sight had been restored. She was gone.

Immediately, I had another lady in front of me wanting prayer for her legs. Back to work.

Jesus tells John's disciples, "Go back and tell John what you have seen and heard, The blind receive sight... "[1] . This is key evidence for John that the Kingdom of God has come, and that Jesus is the promised Messiah. When Jesus reads aloud from the Isaiah scroll in the Nazareth synagogue he proclaims, "He has sent me to proclaim freedom for the prisoners and recovery of sight for the blind." [2]

During those Cwmbran revival days, I would stay close to any blind person to see if they got healed. I wanted to witness someone that was totally blind see again, but I never saw it.

Now I had observed it first-hand. I was elated.

Learning keys

Events in your family, locality, country or even globally, can thwart your ministry plan. If so, ask God what new things he is doing in that season and how you can align with his plans. Look for new opportunities.

Don't let set-backs discourage you. Find a way through. Keep going. Keep praying. Your desire to experience miracles, such as blind eyes seeing, is most likely seeded in you by Jesus. So keep pursuing, even if it may take years to see the first breakthrough.

References

1. Luke 7:22
2. Luke 4:18

8: Like The New Testament Church

"Of dozens of countries I've travelled to and been involved in, very few got me as excited as North Macedonia. I love the apostolic emphasis, boldness, and authentic costly faith."

Simon Guillebaud MBE

Known widely for his missionary work in war-torn Burundi (for which he was awarded the MBE), Simon Guillebaud had temporarily been forced to leave Africa. He had decided to preach his way around the world with his family as part of the children's education. And that brought him to North Macedonia. On one of our Mission Macedonia trips, we landed in the mission house at the same time as Simon, Lizzie and their three children. We teamed up and had great fun together bouncing off each others' energy and ministries.

Simon was amazed by the weekly schedule of the pastors as they visited small churches across the country. He had visited many countries, and he said that this was the closest he had experienced to what the New Testament church would have been like. The church set-up that we support often seems vulnerable, but probably the early church did too. The glue that holds it all together is the pastors and the Holy Spirit.

The Macedonian pastors

We pray hard for Jimmy and his small team of pastors. They are vital to the work there. When any of them become seriously ill, then it becomes a prayer priority for the Mission Macedonia team. The Covid pandemic brought many challenges.

The young pastors, Adams and Marie moved from the capital to live in the poorest village of Red Coast. They have 2 small children. When Adams collapsed with a brain bleed, we were on edge in prayer for weeks as his very survival was touch and go.

Pastor Dabrinka runs the churches out to the East, but travels out to the West too. She works tirelessly. During the pandemic she was weakened for periods of time as she fought off cancer.

Pastors Tefce and Dragona run a farm and have 6 children, including young triplets. Tefce caught Covid and ended up on a ventilator in Skopje. His life hung in the balance as we contested for him daily in prayer. Eventually he came off the danger list, and went home but was suffering from post-Covid fatigue, often called 'Long Covid'. This also impacted his mental health.

On my 2020 trip, Tefce had given me a lift in his car, and we were parked up in Gradsko. I was keen to know how he was. He shared that he still had the chest pains from Covid, a few months after he had been critically ill. I prayed for him as he sat in the car. Listening to God, I sensed that Tefce might have Covid damage to his stomach also, though this was not currently giving him pain. As I prayed, the power of God instantly came on him, then he felt a physical hammer blow on his stomach. I took this as confirmation that there had been a problem there and it was being healed. Next, I prayed for his mind, against all the anxiety. As I did this all the pain went from his chest. When I asked how he now felt, he just replied, 'Super'.

Brothers and church leaders, Alit and Djengis live with their families in the southern city of Prilep. Alit drives a taxi, and Djengis has a long and early commute each day to work in a factory. They both have an untiring heart to share their faith amongst their people, the Roma.

Prilep seems pleasant enough at first sight, but has a reputation for being the most violent city in Macedonia. They showed us the burnt remains of the traditional mosque following a fall-out between the Imam and the Mafia.

The merging of folk magic or witchcraft with an Orthodox or Muslim belief is fairly normal here. Alit had been married at fifteen, still common today, and had been a Muslim Imam before finding faith in Jesus. He shared that, after he became a pastor, he was praying one morning in his home where he led a house church, and felt God lead him into a part of the house that he didn't normally go to. He was prompted to stop where he was and search. Well hidden and wrapped up in clothes was a metal tablet with Arabic etchings that he could not translate. Bewildered, he took the tablet to a Muslim friend who was able to read it. His friend was frightened and told Alit that he should not even be touching the tablet. It was a curse of divorce placed against both his marriage and his brother's marriage, for the family to be broken and separated. The curse was also directed against their parents and their future bloodline. Finally, the invocation was directed against the church in his home, with the intention that it would fall apart. Alit took it, prayed over it and destroyed it. A year later he found out that his own uncle, who was also an Imam, had made the curse. The church continued to grow.

The Roma

Generally North Macedonia is a place where many ethnic groups of different colours seem to rub along nicely together without any racism or prejudice. This does not apply though to the Roma, who are the vulnerable underbelly of society there. They often face both institutional discrimination and social prejudice, often denied education, employment, health provision, or even basic services. Their houses are erected without permissions in shanty villages that can become no-go areas for the police. There were two such villages in rugged mountain locations just outside of Prilep. We became desperate to help them.

Jobbo, Tracey and I went out together in 2021, with pandemic restrictions still in place. We did outreach events with the pastors, in both Roma villages, and combined this with the distribution of much-needed food parcels. At the first village we went to, we set up in a central point near a small shop. I counted over 160 people, including children, filling the streets after we arrived. We worshipped, preached and prayed for people, then repeated this in the second village.

Whilst food distribution was happening, I went for a wander and was welcomed into a home. Three young adults were introduced to me by the man of the house: one son who had pains in his tattooed arm, another who had a serious drugs problem, and finally his wife, a fairer skinned lady, who was unable to have children. He wanted me to pray for them, but I knew my time had run out so suggested they joined us in the Prilep church that night for our special service.

Deep peace

As the service that night drew to a close, the prayer ministry spread from the rented building into the outdoor courtyard where tobacco leaves had been laid out to dry.

It had become evident to us on this trip that everyone being prayed for without exception was being filled with the Holy Spirit, regardless of background or any previous experiences of God. One young lady I prayed for was desperate to see her parents again. After her father had had a row with her husband two years ago, her father had hit him, and her husband was now preventing her seeing her parents. She was very young, and I knew she dreadfully missed her

Mum's hugs. As I prayed for her and her situation, a deep peace from God came upon her; she was swaying, lost in his presence. I let her dwell for some time in the peace of God.

Another young lady of similar age saw this and came up to me. I think she had just walked off the street into the church backyard. She asked me what the girl was doing with her eyes closed and swaying like that. I explained that she was experiencing the presence of God who was helping her and healing her of her hurts. I then asked this girl if she too wanted to experience God's peace and she did. Very soon, she too was soaking in God's presence.

The two young Roma men I had seen in the village were at the service and had followed me out to the back yard, as had a middle-aged lady. I asked the lady to wait a little whilst I prayed for the men.

I did not rush the prayer time and let them soak for a while in the Holy Spirit. Both said the peace of God had swept away their stress and anxiety. The tattooed arm was now pain-free, and the drug addict felt he had changed inside. Time would tell.

Trauma ejected

I then turned to the lady, waiting patiently. She had been suffering from pain in both legs and difficulty in walking for 10 years now. She said that she had being paying doctors for a decade and seen no progress at all. I asked her what had happened 10 years ago, and she replied that this was when her husband died. I knew now that I had to deal with the mental trauma first. As we prayed, she felt the trauma go, as if something was being taken out of her and thrown away. In my mind, I saw a picture of what looked like a scrunched-up ball of iron wool being ejected from her body. She said that she now felt so much lighter.

The trauma was gone, together with its influence on her body. I explained that I could now pray against the pain in her knees and legs. Instantly, as I prayed, all the pain went from her right leg. In that one moment Jesus achieved what 10 years of medical attention had failed to do. However, her other leg was just as painful as before. I prayed for it twice more, by which time the pain had reduced by 50%. I left it there trusting Jesus would finish the healing over the coming days. Do I understand why one leg was fully healed and not the other? No. Do I need to? No.

Hostile womb

At the following day's service, the fair skinned lady from the same home as the Roma men showed up with her husband (the drug addict). We had had prophecies of hostile wombs before we came out; before she spoke I knew this was her problem and she would be healed. She said that her ovaries did not work and she could not have children. I prayed the love of Jesus would flow into her and she was filled with the presence of God. She told me that she could feel an internal heat and then a pulsating in her womb area. Praise God. I then prayed for her with her husband, for a blessing over their marriage and future children.

On a later visit I found that she had given birth three times. Her husband had indeed successfully come off drugs for quite a time, but eventually went back to them and ended up in prison. The wife ran away. It was not clear where the children were.

The more time we spent with the Roma, the deeper our love goes for this very needy people.

Encouraging the youth

One of our biggest joys and priorities in Mission Macedonia has been to encourage the teenagers and young adults. The pandemic had once again prevented the New Hope conference from happening in 2021, but later that year I took my friend Pastor Tim and three young men from my church out for a mission trip.

We started on the first day with street evangelism, using a mixed English and Macedonian team of young people (the youngest was 12 year-old Grace, Pastor Tefce's daughter). Then we gathered together nearly twenty youngsters between the ages of 10 and 25 years old in a large room that is used for services, attached to Dabrinka's house in Obleshevo. We set about some worship, followed by teaching on how to listen to God. We shared testimonies and then had a practical upfront demonstration of getting prophetic words for each other. The Trinity young people excelled in encouraging the Macedonians in this. Grace and her older sister Ruta were first to share what that they had received from God for each other. Then all the youth practiced listening to God and shared their words and pictures in groups of two's and three's.

Later that evening, two 16 year-old twins were asked to share their views on the day. The first said it was the best day of her life, and one she will remember for ever because of the Holy Spirit. When I got back to England, I got a message from the second twin. "I will remember the service in Obleshevo forever. Because that day was wonderful and blessed for me." Wow. It was so encouraging. What a great thing to invest our time and efforts in.

Returning by plane, I found myself chatting with a Macedonian lady now married to a UK pastor. She had found faith as a teenage girl because of a group of Norwegian young people doing evangelism on the streets of the capital Skopje. *What you are doing is so important for our country,* she said. *Keep going. Power to the youth.*

Holy Spirit power, of course.

Learning keys

The Peace of God is very powerful. Pray for it to fill people.

What miracle do you really desire to witness? Pray for that opportunity, and keep praying until you see it.

Whatever your age, young or old, God can use you.

Encourage the next generation. Invest in them. Pass the baton.

9: More Doors Are Opened

An unusual request

It seemed ridiculous at first even to consider the request. Yet I was feeling more and more that God actually wanted me to trust the young pastor in Mombasa, Kenya. God was urging me to go out there. At first, I questioned whether my blessing or anointing (if indeed that is what it was) was maybe just for North Macedonia. Would God use me for healing ministry in another country abroad? I also prefer to be in a team, not working alone.

And the area had a problem with terrorism...

I left my front door in England, genuinely wondering if I would ever see it again.

The corrugated iron place of worship was down a long side track beside a wooden hut labelled *New Hard Rock Café,* a school and a nightclub called *Mtwapa,* after which the whole area was named. Inside, the church was equipped with a stage, keyboard, sound system and speakers two metres high. As I waited for church to start each day, passing school children would shout out 'Jambo, Jambo' at me and laugh loudly, amused by my skin colour.

I spoke 9 times in 8 days. There were three services over two Sundays and then evening meetings on each day in between. These were being advertised as a 'Miracle Revival Conference'. I had never done anything like this before, especially with so much preaching. It was so hot and humid. I had taken a jacket, which lasted one meeting, after which it was short sleeves only, and a 1.5 litre bottle of water for every service. There was a lot of perspiration as the congregation danced hard in the stifling 40C heat during the worship times.

Numbers were nowhere near as high as I had been told they would be, but I could feel a real sense of God's power and presence with me. Despite that, imposter syndrome still came knocking. I pushed it aside. I had been invited and had made myself available. I had the right to be there. I kept telling myself to be bold and confident in Jesus.

I settled into what became a pattern for the week, by getting up to an early morning swim, followed by a light breakfast. Then I spent the day praying and prepping for the evening service, as well as making friends with the motel staff where I could. I was picked up at about 4.30pm each day and returned around 8.30pm. The meetings went well, but although I was careful about what I ate, I got diarrhoea and a throat infection, feeling weaker each day. I pushed on, blocked up by Imodium tablets and soothed by throat lozenges. Despite my own predicament, I still saw people healed daily.

The big difference between Kenya and Macedonia seemed to be the higher visibility of demonic activity. At the final Sunday service one testimony typified this. I remember one larger lady had been there on the Wednesday. She was so overcome by the Holy Spirit when I prayed for her during the worship time, that she was bending over backwards then forwards in quick succession. I wasn't sure if she would fall on her front or back, but she somehow stayed on her feet. In her testimony she said, "I live in a small apartment with my 3 children. My neighbours are heavily into witchcraft and they have sent demons into large rats which run around my apartment at night. I am so fearful of them, I have not been able to sleep at night for more than 2 years. I make sure my children are safe at night, and then I catch up on some sleep during the day. At the revival meeting Pastor Kevin[1] prayed for me, and I was powerfully moved by the Holy Spirit. That night I slept like a baby. My fear has all gone. Each night since, I have slept equally as well, and I give thanks to Jesus for His power."

All change

As I left Nairobi airport, a thermometer gun was pointed at my forehead. There was concern over a virus outbreak which had started in China. This was February 2020. A few weeks later the UK became Europe's Covid hotspot, and I spent the next year working from home. Before I could return to the office, like so many employees I lost my role. I struggled to find another job within the company, so even though I loved my work, I took the option of early retirement. It felt right as I prayed, but I still found it really hard to get used to.

I was reminded of my final term prayer at university. *"Lord Jesus, my next industrial period is not six months, it is forty years. If you do not do something special in my life, I will fall away from faith and you will lose me. If you want to keep me, you need to do something about it".* As I closed that chapter of my life, I could look back and see how he had dramatically answered that prayer in the intervening years. I felt as close to him as I had ever done.

Volunteering in a local coffee shop kept me occupied for a while, but when Pastor Tim asked me to join a trip to Kenya, I jumped at the chance. I was going back to East Africa.

My church, Trinity Cheltenham, has formed an alliance over fourteen years with the diocese of Kericho in Kenya, an area the size of North Macedonia or Wales. Trinity had been invited to come out by the Bishop to deliver a four-day training course for local leaders who would then deliver a discipleship course, called *Rooted in Jesus,* across the diocese. It was hard work but incredible fun to do.

The small ways

God is not just in the headlines but in the details too. Sometimes it is the small things that are the reminders we most need of how he loves us and is looking out for us.

On arrival we ordered a guitar; it had to come from the capital but was due to be delivered the next day at 10.30am. I needed it earlier so opted to drive down to the mail depot at 8.30am, praying that it had been delivered earlier (unheard of in Africa). It was indeed there, waiting.

Centre worker Purity was supposed to be arriving at 4.30pm to lead worship with me using a song she had translated into Masai. At 5.30pm, I was at the front of the meeting with the guitar around my neck looking out over everyone and quietly telling Jesus that I need Purity to arrive in the next 60 seconds. As I was praying this, she walked through the door.

One morning we had no electricity, so it was a cold shower in the dark to start the day. However, we desperately needed some handouts to be photocopied for the first session. We prayed for electricity. Just before the session the power came back on for ten minutes. There was just enough time to do all the photocopying. Then the power promptly went off again.

Coincidences? Trivial issues that would have worked themselves out regardless? William Temple, Archbishop of Canterbury during World War 2, famously commented, “When I pray, coincidences happen, and when I don’t, they don’t.” God is constantly and miraculously at work, in big ways and small, in answer to our prayers. It was true for our team and the local church in Kenya, but is equally true for all of God’s children across the world.

Masai miracles

As well as delivering the training course, our team was asked to lead services across the diocese. So it was that, armed with the afore-mentioned guitar, three of us found ourselves on an hour’s drive down a very bumpy unmade road into the savannah to the church at Oloshaiki. Scattered thorn bushes and occasional trees provided the main distraction from the long dry grass. We were accompanying Pastor Leonard, his wife and his two impeccably dressed young children, Abel and his bigger 8 year-old sister Glorious. The children, I discovered en route, not only spoke good English but could sing the worship song 'Way Maker'.

Oloshaiki was one of several churches in the Olkeri parish for which Leonard was pastor. He explained that the homesteads were very spread out over the parish and some people walked over 30km to church. Apparently the Masai walk fast, and 30km is not a particularly long walk for them.

We arrived early and were greeted by Masai women in vibrant traditional costume. Their green knee-length dresses were decorated with a rich profusion of jewellery, complemented by brightly-patterned material wrapped around their shoulders. Braided hair was tied back into long pony tails.

As visitors, we were welcomed in style: our hands were ceremonially washed and tea was served.

The church was a smart wooden construction with a corrugated metal roof. Soon it started to fill up with the Masai. We decamped to the vestry where Leonard put on his vestments. We might be in a remote part of Kenya where they had never seen a guitar played before, but this was still an Anglican church. Yet it was very much Masai too, with an emphasis on music and traditional dancing, the men, women and youth all taking turns to dance in the generous space allotted at the front of the church. In sharp contrast to the colourful women, the men with few exceptions wore western clothes. Typically, these comprised an open-neck collared shirt and lightweight trousers, with either a non-matching suit jacket, or more casual bomber-style coat.

Luke, one of our team members, gave a testimony, I shared a story on our identity in God, and Helen preached on the parable of the sower. At the end, we did a salvation appeal.

Jackson, a tall Masai man of about 30 years, gave his life to Jesus.

The whole church lined up to shake his hand and warmly welcome him into the Kingdom. Next, the pastor called all of Jackson's family forward for prayer, 16 of them. Later we were told that this was the family that had given the land where the church was built. Now one of their "lost sheep" had come home. An older lady hugged Jackson as tightly as she could; they were both crying. It was his mother.

We had a rest outdoors after the service and took some food with the congregation, but I felt strongly we were not yet finished. I told the Pastor that we did not want to go until anyone with pain or sickness in their bodies had the chance to be prayed for. He took us back to the vestry room and brought us Gladys who had pains in her head, chest and stomach. She had lost people in her life, including a brother who had shot himself. The trauma and fear in her life had become the source of her pain. First, we prayed for inner healing to break off the trauma and fear, and then we prayed out the sickness. All pain went from her head, chest and stomach. She was healed and she left very happy, intent on telling someone.

We were left in the vestry with Pastor Leonard, who then shared his own problem. Back pains had come on suddenly when motor biking through a new area, a month ago. The pain level had stayed steady ever since. This seemed very unusual to me and did not seem to have been caused naturally. He had been riding through a Muslim area at the time, and we deduced that a curse or charm must have been made against him whilst there. First, therefore, we broke the power of the curse in prayer, then prayed out the pain. Later in the week the pastor gave testimony to the training conference of how Jesus had healed his back; the pain had not returned.

Copycat miracles

We were far from finished that day, though. Gladys must have quickly spread the word about her own healing because the Pastor then took us back into the church where a crowd of women were all waiting for us.

The first lady we prayed for, Mary, was the tallest of the traditionally-dressed women who had greeted us on arrival, at around 6 feet 5 inches. She had a stomach ulcer with associated stomach pains, breathing difficulties, chest pains, and severe headaches leading to reduced eyesight. I did my best to listen to what God was saying to me about Mary and deduced that she had a strong spirit of anxiety afflicting her. We ordered the spirit out and then prayed against the sickness. Some pain in the head went and her eyesight was fully restored. We prayed a second time for the rest of head pains but the afflicting spirit was not easily shifted.

I felt Mary needed to sing a line of a worship song three times to get the breakthrough. She sang it twice, but then something was stopping her singing it a third time. We waited but she was unable to sing. I wasn't sure what to do next, then I saw that Glorious, the pastor's young daughter was standing amongst the women. I called her over, got her to place her hand on Mary and asked her to sing, *'Way maker, miracle worker, promise keeper, light in the darkness; my God that is who you are'*. We accompanied Glorious, and as we did Mary's head pains completely went. Next, we prayed for her chest pains which went. Finally, we prayed against her stomach ulcer, and the pains there also went. This had taken a significant time but Mary was eventually healed of all pain and her sight was fully restored.

We asked the next lady amongst the waiting group about her afflictions. They were the same ones that Mary had come with, the head, chest and stomach pains. We then discovered that there were another eight ladies with very similar problems. I asked them about anxiety and they all agreed it applied to them. I had not come across this phenomenon before where a community had been afflicted by the same spirit causing similar illnesses in so many of them. It would have taken too long for us to go through the process for each individually, so after asking God what to do, I felt the Holy Spirit wanted me to get them into a tight group. Our team was to stand around them. We would pray for them all together, in the same way we had done for Mary.

As we did, they were all filled with the Holy Spirit, some falling to their knees. We sensed that whatever spirit had been making the women so anxious had now gone. It was quite a sight as God ministered healing to the whole group. After leaving some more space for the Holy Spirit, I asked for feedback from each. Their differing levels of pain in head, chest and stomach had all been healed. Not one of them said there was more prayer needed in any area at all. It was astonishing. From their feedback, all of them were now completely well. One of the ladies carried on breast-feeding her small child throughout the whole process. It took less time to pray for the whole group to receive their healing than it had for 'tall Mary'.

This was the largest number of confirmed healings that I had ever seen in such a short period of time. It reminded me of when Jesus had told ten lepers to go and see a priest, and all of them were healed of the same affliction when they stepped out in united faith [2]. The oldest lady told me that she could now see much better as her eyes had improved too. I asked if I looked more handsome now, to which she replied that I did; we all laughed. Another miracle.

More than two hours had passed since the end of the service, before we could finally set off back to our base in the rapidly growing and sprawling university town of Narok. Yet Pastor Leonard had one more request. Could we stop off on our way back to pray for one of his parishioners who had been too sick to come that day?

Joseph Joy

We drove across open countryside until we came to a simply constructed building with scarcely any windows. It was pretty dark as we entered the room where the patient lay.

Joseph Joy was diabetic. He had already had half his left leg amputated. Swelling and pain in his right leg and foot was preventing him attending worship services, as he was now unable to walk. There was a real danger he might lose this second leg. Pastor Leonard explained that we had insufficient time to accept drinks and discuss the customary pleasantries, which can generally take an hour or so. Unusually, therefore, we plunged right into praying into his illness. This was a big prayer.

At first sight, it did seem that without a miracle it would not be long before a second amputation was needed. However, when we prayed, we could sense the Holy Spirit on him and Joseph told us there was a change in his right leg. We had no way to verify this but he seemed very happy to put his weight on it. Though it was clear to us he was not completely healed, he was able to get up and walk to see us out, with the help of a stick and his prosthetic limb. Some progress definitely seemed to have been made.

There were so many amazing experiences on our Kenya trip that I am afraid I never gave Joseph Joy another thought. Nine months later, I had the opportunity to return to Narok and do more with the ACK (Anglican Church in Kenya).

An exciting and immensely worthwhile farm field school was to be launched at the church in Olkeri, one of the congregations overseen by Pastor Leonard. It was so good to be reunited with him and his family again. We were also introduced to the farmers whose way of living would be transformed out of all recognition by the project.

Then Leonard announced that someone had made a journey especially to see me. A large gentleman wearing a floppy domed and brimmed hat walked confidently up to the church. It took a few moments for me to realise who it was, but then the penny dropped. Here, walking towards me with head held high was Joseph Joy, beaming from ear to ear. His leg had completely healed. Presumably his diabetes had gone. I hugged his large frame several times. Later I closely observed him walking down a slope to the stream, just to be doubly sure that his health was restored. He did great.

What a surprise! What joy! God is so good.

Learning keys

When Jesus calls you and you respond, he will give you the tools you need, to do the job he has asked.

Take delight in the small answers to prayer, not just the big ones.

God's healing power may continue in a person long after you have left and forgotten about your prayer.

References

1. In many parts of Africa, it is quite normal to call a lay person Pastor if they are engaged in evangelism or teaching

2. Compare Luke 17:12-17

10: Winning On Home Turf

The previous chapters compact a whole lifetime into a few pages. Maybe it sounds from them that I was never at home. In fact, my trips abroad before early retirement occupied no more than two to four weeks a year. For the remaining 11 months I was at home, living on the edge of town, working full-time, bringing up a family and keeping my old car going as long as possible. If I travelled to speak in other churches, I rarely went far.

The vast majority of my time has always been spent on home turf. This will be true for most readers too. Let's start where we are, but move out further if we are called.

Church

Jesus did healing ministry in his local synagogue. So what about my own local church? What about yours? Shouldn't that be a place of healing too?

Having spent most of my life in small non-conformist churches, I now go to a lively Anglican church where there are a whole lot of people who care passionately about Christ's Kingdom, and who work in faith and in the power of the Holy Spirit to bring that Kingdom to their friends and neighbours. Evening services are simple, with three sections each lasting about half an hour. There is worship, the word preached, and ministry time. Interestingly there is no 'prayer time' where someone leads the congregation in prayers from the front. Instead, the prayers happen one on one at the front of the church. Off the back of the message, people are asked to respond by coming forward and bringing their needs to Jesus. Someone from the church family will come alongside and pray for each person that comes forward. Often it is a case of simply asking the Holy Spirit to come and do what he needs to do. *More love, more power, Lord.*

Sometimes the minister will call to the front anyone who needs healing in their body. This gives a great opportunity to practice healing prayers in a safe space. Recently after one of the pastors made the invitation, I ended up praying with three people one after the other (I would normally pray for only one person during this time). First, Josh had a rugby injury caused by someone having fallen on his neck; he was in a lot of pain. Second, Will had been experiencing pains in his back and chest for over a month. After prayer, both said the pains had gone. Then I prayed for Luke, who was getting intermittent fluttering sensations in his chest. As the Holy Spirit came, he felt the tension go in his chest and believed he had been healed.

The following week, Charlie came forward. He showed me his broken and swollen finger. It might sound a small thing, but it still required a miracle. I had never prayed for a broken finger, or a broken toe for that matter. Doubt is never far from your mind when you step out to do healing ministry, especially if it's for something you've not seen healed before. You have to push through the doubt. As we prayed, the Spirit came; the swelling and the pain both went and the finger was healed.

The benefit of in-church ministry is that you generally get to see the person again. Five days later we were both at a teaching session on spiritual gifts where Charlie shared with the group about his healing miracle. It takes two to tango. Charlie had to first step out boldly to the front for prayer, then someone had to step up to pray for him. If one of us had held back, then no miracle.

If your church has more of a traditional service and does not yet have space for healing ministry, then find someone else like-minded who is happy to pray for others. Talk it through with your church leaders and invite them to go on this new journey with you. Weekly ministry will probably be too a big step at the start, but even a monthly prayer time would be good. It might be helpful to invite people to stay behind immediately after the service, if they want prayer for healing. We all have to start somewhere and church is a good place to start.

Whether we need our own healing, want more supernatural ability from God, or want to use that power to see specific miracles, we need to take a brave step forward, ask God, and persist for the breakthrough.

Sometimes, though, we're in no fit state to take any initiative ourselves. We depend on the faith of others. My editor and friend Richard shared with me his own story of God's power through a church worker who stepped out of church to do healing prayer.

"I still vividly remember the paramedics precariously stretchering me down a steep flight of stairs from our flat. I could hardly speak or move, let alone stand. It was late Friday afternoon but the consultant hurried back to hospital to examine me. There was something that felt like a knife-wound inside my lower back as he angled the ultrasound scanner screen towards me, revealing a 2.5 cm cist on my liver, potentially life-threatening. Through the searing pain I heard him telling me that I would need enormous doses of antibiotics, intravenously administered. It would be a long haul.

Over the weekend, a church youth worker visited my hospital bed, anointed me with oil[1] and prayed for me. I didn't feel any different but I was glad he had come. On Monday morning, however, the consultant did another ultrasound scan and was astonished to see the cist had shrunk by 75%. He showed me the screen again and I could see the difference right in front of me. *'I think we can call that...* (he paused)... *remarkable.'* I was discharged by the end of the week and back at work a fortnight later."

Small groups

I'm also greatly blessed by being part of a small group of local Christians who we pray together, encourage each other and listen for what the Holy Spirit is saying. We come together regularly. It's fun, we sometimes eat together, we study together a little, but we prioritise time for praying and prophesying over each other.

Picture maybe 6 or 8 of us meeting in a friend's sitting room. After eating, we may study the Bible for a while. Perhaps we will focus on passages relating to the gift of prophecy, then we'll take it in turns to be prayed over. When it is my turn to be prayed for, I stand still, eyes closed, hands out in 'receive mode' and resist the temptation to speak. Often, I start my mobile phone voice recorder, so I can capture what is said.

The others will pray quietly and listen to God, asking for words or pictures for me which they will then share. This is alway kept positive and encouraging. Let someone else do the gloom and doom stuff.

My friends may have an interpretation of what the pictures or words mean, or they may not. Often, the words will be similar, which encourages everyone. Not everything will be accurate. As the apostle Paul wrote, "We know in part, and we prophesy in part".[2] Later I can sift through prayerfully what has been shared, and reject what I feel may be false.

If someone in the group is sick or anxious, then we pray for them to be healed during that time. It is all good practice, and this is a safe space. I also keep a journal to write up the prophecies and healings I've witnessed or experienced.

Even if your church activities do not currently offer practical support in the gifts God is developing in you, look for others in whom the Holy Spirit is at work in prophecy or healing. Essentially, a small group can be a training ground for you.

Festival time

A life without festival is a long road without an inn. (Democritus of Abdera)

The annual New Hope festival in North Macedonia has a unique place in my heart. To be in a team that organises these events where we see so many people blessed, saved and healed, has been both exhilarating and humbling. But I am also blessed by some of the numerous Christian festivals that take place annually in the UK. There is something very empowering in celebration. The intensity of so much prayer and worship going up in a single place, impacts the atmosphere. I love being there. They can be wonderful places not just to hear testimonies of miracles from those healed, but to see miracles as they happen. Sometimes you can have a go yourself.

I always try to get into the main celebration early and bag a place near the front. I try to get distractions out of my mind, focus on God and soak it all in. When the ministry team is praying for healings, there can be an opportunity to be somewhere in the mix. Each time that I do see someone healed, my faith steps up more than a notch.

A good friend called Helen told me of an occasion she went to at a youth festival. At that time, she had one leg about two inches shorter than the other, and her body was compensating. Her back was twisted with one hip lower than the other, which gave her persistent pain. One day, the speaker, Mark Marks, said he had a word for a girl called Helen; she had a back problem and God wanted to heal it. Helen went forward.

In her own words… "He sat me on a chair, and stretched my two legs out in front of me. He prayed for me with 700 young people watching and a video recording it. He said, 'Helen, Jesus loves you, you're his daughter.' Then he prayed out loud, 'In the name of Jesus, leg grow, back straighten and strengthen.' It then felt like someone was pulling my leg. I looked and he was not touching anywhere near my ankle or leg, but it still slowly pulled forward. I could feel that sensation of it being pulled. I then stood up and put my hands on my hips so everyone could see levels, and they had evened up perfectly. The constant niggling low pain that I had felt for years and years had completely gone. You can clearly see the miracle on the video that was taken."

Festivals are great.

Thin walls

I periodically stay at a Christian retreat centre in the Gwaun Valley, a remote but beautiful part of West Wales. It has the reputation of being a 'thin place' where God often moves in blessings and miracles. Some people go there as a last resort, having tried everything else. Many have been there and come away with what they had wanted from God, including dramatic healing miracles.

On an early visit, I remember being asked by Anna, who worked there, if I wanted to start my stay with a blessing. I agreed and we went into the small domed lime-washed chapel. She spoke a blessing over me in her wonderful Welsh accent, and the words came across with so much power I was almost knocked off my feet.

Jesus often took himself off to a remote spot alone to do business with his Father God, and get empowered for his ministry. Perhaps he had some favourite spots. For many, people being close to nature brings them close to God. In one sense God is with us wherever we go but look out for actual places and buildings with what I call 'thin walls'.

My Christian retreat centre in Wales is definitely one of those 'thin wall' places for me. If God leads me there for two or three days, I do expect to see miracles at some point during my stay, but my main motivation in coming is to pray, and have that focussed prayer time. I sense that these times empower me in some way for future ministry.

These places may take some finding, but it is worth the effort. They are invaluable retreats for seeing breakthrough in your life, and are usually worth travelling a long way for. Even though I live reasonably close to the Welsh border, it is a four-hour drive. Most people travel much further to this remote but beautiful spot. Twice, for example, I have met visitors from Norway.

The power of worship

I love worshipping God and have recently picked up my guitar again. I have come to learn that there is real power in sung worship, which seems to me to be equally as powerful as prayer. In fact, I am no longer sure where worship ends and prayer starts.

On one occasion, King David was having the Ark of the Covenant taken to Jerusalem. There were trumpets and shouts of joy en route. David was wearing just a linen cloth, and dancing to God for all he was worth. On arrival, David had a tent set up for the Ark, where the presence of God would now dwell.[3] He was criticized for his semi-naked dancing but he didn't care. He said he was prepared to look even more ridiculous than that, to put God first and praise him. I like that.

A highlight for me in recent years has been a festival called *David's Tent*. A big marquee provides the venue for 72 hours of non-stop worship music. There are some big names involved, singers and bands, but no-one is announced or cheered off. The sets transition one into another. The focus remains on God. Just as I feel empowered through my prayer retreats in Wales, so, in the same way, the Holy Spirit meets us through this worship weekend. I feel a need to worship with all my might like David did. No surprise, I will be near the front and keep going as long as I can. Why? First because Jesus deserves all our praise, but also there is a return. There is no formula to this, but I feel the more I give out in worship, the more I receive in blessing. There is an empowering in those times which I can give out when on mission abroad. I need to worship.

It was during a worship time that I had my most powerful encounter with the Holy Spirit. I had already been there for over 12 hours and had almost left twice earlier, but talked myself into staying longer. It was in my final hour that I felt a power shaking and moving me in ways I find hard to describe. What I did know, was that when he finished, he had done something deep within me, leaving me feeling bolder and more confident in my Christian walk and ministry.

Mission trips

The visible part of a mission trip takes place overseas, but the key prayer and preparation times take place mostly on home turf. Then, when we step out, lives are changed.

On the final day of each mission trip to North Macedonia, everyone shares their own personal experiences. Though we always come in order to give out to the Macedonians, each of us discovers by the end of the trip that we've actually received even more in return. For some of the team that week's experience will transform their lives for ever.

A few weeks ago, I didn't know why I was on the team; what could God do with me in Macedonia? a first-timer will say. Now the team sits around the crowded lounge in the Mission House giving amazing testimonies of what they had seen done.

Ellie is just one example, a young graduate working in the Insurance business. She had been praying with us for over a year and was developing prophetic gifting, but could not see how Jesus could use her. She first came out for New Hope 2019 and teamed up with Trudie who had recently started praying for people for healing.

"How did it go, Ellie?" I asked after the conference.

"Eyes, three different people healed of eye problems. Lots of pains like in heads, backs and knees gone or reduced. One demon-possessed lady we prayed for was released from it, and we prayed for three or four people to accept Jesus in their lives for the first time".

These nervous, doubting volunteers come home brimming with confidence and excitement, as they have seen first-hand God use them in miraculous ways.

If you want to learn to see miracles, get involved with a group that expects to see God move in power, in the supernatural, whether it's in your local church, elsewhere in the UK, or on an overseas mission trip. God wants to challenge you, encourage you and expand your understanding of how he's working today.

Seize the day

The point of this chapter, however, is that local ministry was the starting point for Jesus. It was where he returned often. Wherever we are, there will be opportunities to serve God. We just need to seize them.

Gilbert was an internationally acclaimed classical guitarist who had played the BBC Proms in the Royal Albert Hall London, and had been resident in my village for a long time. I had known him for over 30 years, when I met him one day in the changing rooms of a local leisure centre. He had suffered a stroke and was struggling to get dressed. I felt the Holy Spirit saying to me, *Invite him out for coffee.* God clearly wanted to do something, so I was particularly glad that Gilbert readily accepted my suggestion. We soon got onto the topic of faith and why some like me believed in God, and others like Gilbert did not.

"Now you have a strong faith, Kevin," Gilbert said, "you've got it all sewn up, haven't you? You don't need to ask any more questions."

I disagreed with him, and explained that I had never stopped asking questions. "Yes, I believe in God, and I believe his Word through the Bible is the truth. What I don't believe is that my interpretation of what I have experienced and what I have read is always right. I don't align myself with those who feel that their interpretation of the Gospel must be right, and everyone else must therefore be wrong. They've tied God to a set of rules based on their own personal experience to date. They aren't open to new revelation, much like the Pharisees weren't."

I told my friend that my faith was a journey and not a destination, a journey that I hope will never finish, in this world or the next. I want to make the most of each day and keep learning more about God. What we were able to agree on was that every day was a precious gift.

At that moment for some reason, I mentioned the film *Dead Poets Society*. It turned out that Gilbert loved it.

In the film, we remembered, the college students are surprised by the unorthodox teaching methods of their new English teacher John Keating (played by the marvellous Robin Williams), who encourages his students to 'make your lives extraordinary.'

"He uses that phrase *Carpe Deum*," I enthused.

"No, it's *Carpe diem*," smiled the world-renowned guitarist. "*Carpe diem* means 'seize the day.' What you've just said is Latin for 'seize God'."

Suddenly we both stopped talking and looked at each other. It was a light-bulb moment. What if they were the same? What if you seize the day by seizing God and placing him right in the middle of your everyday problems and challenges?

Everywhere you look there are people who are trapped by addiction, those who are depressed, or caged by fear, and many who are physically or mentally sick. You will know someone who has regular migraines, or persistent back-pain. Each could be helped by a supernatural act of God. You are 'the Christian'. There is no need to go abroad to see miracles.

The Ongoing Journey

I am still work in progress. I still have to remember to "seize God" every day. I am hoping there are a lot more adventures to go on, and many more miracles to see.

But with this chapter, you're now up to date with where I am at. In the next section I want to look in more detail at what we can learn about miracles and how to see them. God is calling you on a journey too. Let's go exploring together.

Learning keys

Ask God for opportunities to pray for sick people, for those you live and work amongst.

Where possible, pray for someone where they are, at the moment they ask for prayer.

Make space in your local church services for healing ministry, and get involved.

Book into Christian festivals which minister in the supernatural power of the Holy Spirit. Get in the mix.

Stay and pray at a Christian retreat centre, where the presence of God is very evident.

Be a lover of worship, and use it to help usher in the power of God.

Join or form a small group, as a safe space for learning about and practising gifts of the Spirit.

Join a local group that has a passion for mission, then go on a mission trip.

References

1. James 5:14

2. 1 Corinthians 13:9

3. 2 Samuel 6

PART 2
THE LEARNING

11: Ready For The Off

The starting gate

Greyhounds are naturally aerodynamic and their narrow frame coupled with powerful back legs makes them perfect for sprinting. They are born with the instinct to chase and can reach speeds of up to 45 miles per hour. To race, they need to be prepared well, but the day will eventually come when they are ready for the off. The dog is led into the starting gate from the rear and through a small window can see the track and the mechanical rabbit. When all dogs are in the right position, the gates swing upward to release the dogs. This is the moment of truth: will your dog stay in the starting gate, or will it follow its instincts and training to run the race?

As a follower of Jesus, you are a new creation, adopted into his family. You are designed exactly as the maker wanted, to be an ambassador for Christ. Now with the Holy Spirit living in you, you are equipped for the task ahead: fighting evil, bringing the supernatural kingdom of God into the everyday world, shining his light in the darkness, and seeing miracles. But will you leave the starting gate? Will you run the race set before you?

Having taken you on my journey, I'd like to help you step out further on your own.

First, we will look at the need to be open to miracles, to make ourselves available, and to learn to listen to God for directions. Then we will look at all the main tools that we have already been given, to help us succeed in our life-long mission.

Whilst this book focuses on healing miracles, I also want to take a look some other miracles, such as the miracle of forgiveness, creation miracles, and raising the dead.

Finally, I want to offer up some practical instructions on praying for healing, before sending you on your way to see miracles for yourself. Let's get going.

Be open

God does spiritual things. Of course he does. He's supernatural. We know that. But do we expect him to do visible things which sometimes go against the normal laws of nature? Jesus' Parable of the Sower [1] shows that there will always be a range of responses to his promises:

- *Some just won't believe anything unless they see it with their own eyes.* (This scepticism might be strengthened by the teaching that "miracles just don't happen today".) Thomas felt like this when his fellow disciples said they had seen Jesus risen from the dead. Jesus then appeared to his friend and told him to stop doubting. [2] Jesus then commented to Thomas, "Blessed are those who have not seen and yet have believed." (i.e. he expects us to trust the reliable testimony of others). Just because you haven't seen a miraculous healing yet, does not mean that you won't see it very soon.

- *A lot of Christians believe in the principle that miracles occur, but do not expect to see any.* They may have a real problem with unanswered prayer; perhaps they endured great disappointment and pain when a loved one has died after much prayer. We explore unanswered prayer in a later chapter. There are sound reasons why not everyone is healed (whether through supernatural miracles or through medical technology), but that does not make either supernatural healing or medical technology any less real.

- *Sadly, there are cases of falsified miracles.* Whilst counterfeits may happen, this is not evidence against the real thing. A counterfeit banknote does not mean that real ones do not also exist.

- *Some may not see miracles because they demand them from God for the wrong reasons.* Perhaps they want the acclaim of being called a miracle worker, or they think they know much better than God how things should work out. "Those who exalt themelves will be humbled, and those who humble themselves will be exalted."[3]

- *Finally, some will not accept miracles, even if they see them happen.* They will find a reason or excuse why the miracle could have occurred naturally. If nothing else, it can be dismissed as a mere coincidence. People may claim that it is impossible to believe in miracles "in this modern scientific age."

Scepticism is nothing new. Jesus certainly met the fiercest of sceptics. In the Bible, divine signs are noticed by those who are open, but bring hostility out in those who reject them. Some that saw the Jesus' miracles got so angry with him that they plotted to kill him.[4]

What all the above examples show us is that the first step in seeing miracles is to be open to them. Then, when miracles happen, they get our attention and redirect us to the wonder of God. Remember the Bible frequently uses the term "signs and wonders" to describe miracles. They are by definition out of the ordinary. If they happened all the time, then we might assume that was just the way of nature, and not see God at work.

Be available

God only uses one type of people: those who make themselves available to him.

In the Old Testament, the prophet Isaiah is caught up in a vision of God [5]. There is a job to be done, a message to be taken to the people of Israel, and he hears the voice of God say "Whom shall I send? Who will go for us?" Isaiah replies, "Here am I, send me." God responds, "Go, and tell this people."

My solo trip to Mombasa had been a full-on experience which was hard to assimilate. Why had Jesus taken me all that way to work amongst a few Kenyans? On my last day, I asked God that question as I prayed, and immediately a reply came to me. *'There was a job which needed doing. There are not many available workers to me. You were available, so I sent you.'*

Seems fair enough when you put it like that.

Make yourself available to God, even if it's not convenient. Be prepared to say, 'Here I am Lord, send me.'

Embrace the moment

When you make yourself, your time and your finances available to Jesus, it is game on. Anything can happen, at any time. The disciples were gathered in an upper room, 50 days after the resurrection, and suddenly the Holy Spirit descended on them in what sounded like wind and looked like fire. [6] It was sudden.

Desire the 'suddenly moments'.

I was on a short walk to my evening service one Sunday, when I came across a commotion on a street corner. The lady was very distressed. Her mobility scooter had broken down. I knew I was supposed to help. For the next hour, I pushed her scooter back to where she lived, with her walking slowly and holding on to me. I was able to share my faith on that journey and pray for her after getting her home. I missed going to church, but did not miss living out church to someone in need. I had embraced the moment.

Walking back, I felt convicted, not for missing church, but for all the times that I had not embraced the moment. I needed to listen more to God and respond to his prompts when he sends those 'suddenly moments'.

Learn to listen

If you ask what has been the most significant change in my Christian journey over recent years, I would reply it has been starting to make more effort to listen to God.

When I visited the monastery at Kicevo in Macedonia I fell into conversation with a young nun, Sister Nicolette. She was wearing the traditional black habit, with a head covering that swept down over her shoulders. Her face was lively, bright and inquisitive.

"What are you doing in the area?" she enquired. I explained that my Macedonian companion Darko and I were listening to God's voice. We would go where we felt sent that day, and take whatever ministry opportunity was made available.

"Only a priest can hear God's voice," Sister Nicolette tried to explain.

"Can we look at the Bible together?" I asked. When she agreed, I went on: "Jesus says 'My sheep listen to my voice, I know them, and they follow me'.[7] There is no singular lead sheep referred to here. Jesus is talking about his entire flock of followers, all who put their trust in him. It's no different today. God always has something to say to all of us, but most of the time we are not listening."

The young nun looked bemused but did not argue; it had given her food for thought.

The big question though is: *How do I hear God's voice?*

We are all different, and the ways that God communicates with us will vary. A few people at times hear an audible voice. Others have vivid dreams, or like Isaiah they get caught up in a vision. These people are in the minority though. For most of us, the experience will probably be a lot more subtle.

The butterfly

A thought drops into your mind. It may be there just for a moment and then it's gone. It is like a butterfly landing on a leaf, then flying off. It is not an audible voice, and it is not usually an insistent voice in your head. For me at least, God's voice is generally sudden, gentle and fleeting. It gets my attention. I recognise first that this is not coming from my normal ongoing thoughts (i.e. it is not about work, shopping, football or whatever). I may have been intentionally listening out for God, but not necessarily. Then I need to tune into that idea, recognise who it is from, and focus on it. What is God trying to tell me? What does he want me to do about it? When?

Having said all this, I have occasionally heard God's voice being very insistent indeed. He may want me to do something fairly urgently and I am not immediately complying. I once had that persistent voice in my head for days until I finally gave in and did it.

The snatcher

I found that the first "voice" (or idea) is often closely followed by a second one in my head. This second voice will either contradict the first, or it will cast doubts on what I have heard. *Don't turn left, turn right. Don't go and take those flowers to your sick neighbour; she would be embarrassed. Don't be silly; God would never ask you to do that. You are just making things up.*

My rule of thumb is that the first voice that has landed is God's, and the second is my spiritual enemy trying to prevent me from doing what God wants. Paul warned the church in Corinth about this [8]. Protect that first 'still small voice' against anything that your body or mind is telling you, anything that would stop you being obedient to God.

It may not always be the case, but when I follow that first voice and ignore the second, it usually turns out to be exactly right.

Dreams

Perhaps God will speak to you in dreams. We see numerous examples of this in the narrative of Jesus' birth, when Mary's fiancée Joseph hears three times from God in a dream[9]. It was a popular belief back then that the three signs of God favour of your life were "a good king, a fruitful year, and a good dream." So the fact that these announcements came in three dreams made Joseph very open to accepting them as coming from God. He took Mary as his wife, fled from Herod in time, and returned when he knew Herod was dead, all because of dreams.

I have not as yet heard from God in dreams. To be honest, I hardly ever wake up remembering a dream. That's me. Some of my friends, though, are regularly spoken to in this way. So give it a go. Offer up your dream life and ask God to speak to you through it. Journal as soon as you wake. If you are hearing in this way, then ask God for interpretations of your dream if they are not obvious. Find others to whom God speaks in dreams and learn from them, but also look for resources that will help you in your interpretation. You will learn what different images, numbers and colours mean. If it is for you, then it is an exciting way to hear God's words for your life.

Bible open prayers

Ask God to speak to you through his Word. This is one of the most common ways he speaks to us. Let him guide you to passages through your thoughts. Pray with your Bible open. A well-worn Bible with lots of underlining is helpful in homing in on key passages that Jesus wants to speak to you through. When you are in a passage, then meditate on it. *Lord what are you telling me through this passage?* Then pray into it.

Try and memorize Bible passages, and let God bring them to the front of your mind when you need them. I wish I was better at this.

Be alert in the moment

Practice hearing from God in your personal prayer times and small groups, but also be alert to God's voice when you are out and about. Practise by asking him, *Lord, do you want to speak to me in this situation? Was that a butterfly that just landed?*

Jesus spent a lot of time with his Heavenly Father in wilderness places, praying and listening. It was like his morning spiritual gym workouts, equipping him for the day ahead. Then he would be ready for whatever came his way; a wedding which runs out of wine, his boat almost sinking in a storm, a paralyzed man let down through a roof. At any time, he is ready to say the right word, or do the miracle that is required. He seized God the Father. He seized the power of the Spirit. He seized the moment.

Harriet Tubman

After her own escape from slavery in Maryland USA, Harriet Tubman, became a key player in the 'underground railroad' that rescued others from slavery. Slave owners put a huge ransom on her head, yet she confidently and consistently avoided pursuers and patrols by listening to God's voice. She always asked God what to do and let him direct her path. It was said of her that she would talk about 'consulting with God' just as one would consult a friend upon matters of business.[10] "I always told him, I trust you. I don't know where to go or what to do, but I expect you to lead me. He always did.'[11] In the American Civil War, she was commissioned to lead a military assault which freed more than 700 slaves. She went on to fight for Women's Rights, always following God's voice.

Unblock my ears

In 2016, I went forward for prayer at my own church because I wanted to hear God's voice better. During this time, both the man praying for me and I got the same picture in our minds. It was of my ears being syringed and lumps of wax coming out. In that moment I felt the weight of God's presence and the sense that I would have a clearer voice from God in my head; I would have a stronger prophetic gifting. Soon after, I started up the Mission Macedonia prayer meetings, and began the journey of following his voice more closely.

For Example...

Here are some simple examples of hearing God's voice from my own journey.

Let God tell you.

We were leading an outreach service in Macedonia when Jimmy pointed the man out to Jason and me.

"I want you both to pray for that man, but I am not going to tell you what his problems are," Jimmy announced. "Let God tell you." We obediently prayed and listened. Different words dropped into each of our minds. We agreed God was telling us that the man had an addiction, but we disagreed what it was.

"Okay," I smiled at Jason. "You go first".

The man agreed with Jason that he did indeed have a problem with alcohol. A big problem. We prayed against the addiction. Then, when we finished, I said to the man in a deliberately quiet voice, "Can I ask, is it possible that you are also looking at some images that you should not be?" A knowing smile split his face, and he replied in a loud voice, which the whole church could have heard. "Yes, pornography."

Bad finger nails

One man who came forward for prayer, wanted his finger nails to be better. Basically, they had all disintegrated. I knew straight away that Jesus would not heal him *physically* that day. Instead, I asked him about his faith. "I believe in God," he confessed, "but I'm no longer walking with him." I asked him if he would like to rededicate himself to Jesus. "Yes," he replied. So I took him through a prayer of recommitment and prayed for the Holy Spirit to pour into him and keep him on the right lines. I then had a word from God: the man was now to use his hands to serve God. As he did this, then and only then would his hands be restored. Often in these situations, you have no way of knowing if your prophetic words are accurate or not, because you may never see the person again. But all I can do is listen to the faint voice and stirrings and speak out what I believe at the time. That day, what he needed most was not new finger nails, but Jesus in his life. I led him to Jesus. He left blessed.

The honey jug

During New Hope 2019, I was about an hour into my prayer queue, when a lady told me that she had pain everywhere; head, body, arms, legs, feet, everywhere. It was probably fibromyalgia. "Wow," I said, "well let's see what Jesus wants to do for you today." I spent a moment quietly checking in with Jesus and listening for instructions. He asked me to pray over the top of her head and invite the Holy Spirit to flow through her from top to bottom. As I did this, the Spirit gave me a picture in my mind of her, with a gigantic jug of honey being poured over her from above, dripping down over her body, covering her with sweet goodness. Images like this are how I hear most frequently from God. In that moment I knew that, whatever was wrong with her, she was going to be totally healed. With my hands on her head, I prayed the Spirit to come in love and power over her. As I did, I could sense the power on her, and she could feel her whole body warm up with the Spirit's touch from top to bottom, until her whole body was tingling with the Spirit's presence. I waited a little then checked in with her. All her pain had gone. Every bit of it. Thanks, Jesus.

The giggler

In 2022, we finally got the New Hope conferences going again, with more than 200 delegates from across the country squeezed onto the Veles HQ balcony. There were so many great blessings and stories from that time, but one in particular makes me smile.

During a ministry time I sensed one teenage girl wanted prayer

> but was unsure about coming forward, so I called her over. She had pains in her wrist, forearm and shoulder. I prayed first for the Holy Spirit to bless her, then on listening to God, I felt I should ask her an unusual question. "Do you like telling jokes?" "Yes," she replied, then started giggling. It was infectious, and spread to those of us praying with her. We laughed in the Spirit for a few minutes. When we had calmed down, I asked her how her wrist was. The pain had gone, not only in her wrist but in her forearm too. We had not even prayed for them yet. Even her shoulder was nearly back to normal.

Listen to God and seek his guidance in whatever way you can. Few things are more important, whether you're praying for someone's healing, or setting off to your workplace in England, or going to school in America.

How can you always hear God 100% accurately, and never make mistakes? You can't, but don't let that stop you. We learn from our mistakes. Paul told the church in Corinth that we only see God's purposes for us like a poor reflection in the mirror. When we are with him in eternity we will understand in full, but for now we only know in part.[12]

Lord, I am listening, what do you want to say to me today? It is good to make that a daily prayer.

Learning keys

Put aside scepticism, and embrace the possibility of miracles. Be open, and look for them.

Make yourself available to God. If you do, he will use you.

Take time to listen to God. Learn the art of listening. Discern what promptings are from God, which are your own thoughts, and which ones are planted by your spiritual enemy. (These often come immediately after God's words and say the opposite).

Try opening up your dreams to hearing from God. Journal your dreams, and seek interpretations.

You will make mistakes, but don't let that stop you. Learn from them.

References

1. Matthew 13:1-23
2. John 20:24-29
3. Matthew 23:12
4. John 11:45-57
5. Isaiah 6
6. Acts 2:1-4
7. John 10:27
8. 2 Corinthians 10:5
9. Matthew 1:20, 2:13 and 2:19
10. Robert Clemens Smedley, History of the Underground Railway in Chester and the Neighbouring Counties of Pennsylvania, Andesite Press, 2017
11. Robert C Plumb, The Better Angels, Nebraska: Pontomac Books Inc, 2020
12. 1 Corinthians 13:12

12: The Spiritual Toolbox

People are hungry for purpose in their lives. When I lost my manager's role during the pandemic, what hit me most was the loss of purpose that my every day routine gave me. I needed to remind myself that my identity and purpose is not from man; it is not even from a vocation. My purpose comes from the Lord.

We are given purpose as disciples of Jesus, to live for him, to see his kingdom come on earth as it is in heaven. We need to pursue that purpose. Our loving Father God promises that if we seek, we shall find; if we knock, the door will be opened. [1]

If you are looking to step out in faith and see miracles, you are not starting from scratch. As a follower of Jesus, you are already well equipped.

We were in a Muslim town with a reputation for being radical, but were in one of just three homes which identified as Orthodox Christian. A tree had once fallen on the older brother, damaging his shoulder and spine. There had been some recovery, but he still experienced weakness and pain in his back. I so wanted our time of prayer to be life-changing for the family. I was desperate for them to see God's power at work.

He stood in front of us ready to receive from Jesus, with all the family watching. The second that we started to pray, the Muslim call for prayer rang out from the mosque like a challenge to us. It felt, however, that we were in that peaceful place in the eye of the storm. God was with us.

I had no first aid kit with me and no medical training, but what I did have with me was all I needed, my spiritual toolbox. Invisible but real. We prayed three times; the pain reduced, diminished further, and then was gone.

God has given us what we need to engage with his power. So let's have a closer look at what is actually available to us as we step out and pursue his purposes. What is in our spiritual toolbox?

#1 The Holy Spirit

"I am the vine; you are the branches. If you remain in me and I in you, you will bear much fruit; apart from me you can do nothing."[2] Jesus paints a picture that leaves no room for doubt. You are one of the branches. As long as you stay connected to the vine which is Jesus, then you get sap from the vine, the Holy Spirit. The Spirit produces good fruit in us: love, joy, peace, patience, kindness, goodness, faithfulness, gentleness and self-control. [3] And it is also through this connectedness that we get the spiritual gifts and the power to see miracles. We need to realise just how generous our loving Father is. He wants to gift us good things.

I was once at a talk, after which the lady speaker invited anybody forward that wanted to receive for the first time the gift of tongues. "If you already speak in tongues but want another language, then also come up," she added. About a third of us did, and we all received a gift from God. I had not even realised you could get more than one spiritual tongue until that day. The big question I was left with, though, was why the others in the room did not come forward. They went home without a gift.

I think we should ask, ask and ask God for more of the spiritual. I do not think it upsets him one iota. In fact, I think it pleases him. In Paul's list [4], the likes of tongues, prophetic words, healing the sick and other miracles are all up for grabs. These gifts did not cease after Luke wrote the book of Acts. They are very much alive and kicking and should be on your bucket list.

Paul urges the Corinthians to "desire the spiritual gifts".[5] A good translation would be to *fervently and consistently plead with passion* for spiritual gifts from God. A gift is not an entitlement, so we are not guaranteed the gifts we ask for. Ask anyway. Chase them down. Don't give up. It really is okay.

Wouldn't it be weird for a mother or father if their children never asked for anything? We give generously, but of course we don't hand over everything they ask for. Sometimes they have to keep asking and wait a bit, but if we love our children, we actually want to give them good things. Everything God the Father has to offer us is good. Ask. Receive.

If you have received spiritual gifts, then use them regularly. I am amazed by how many people have received gifts from God, then put them away. They are intended for use in the spiritual battlefield, not to gather dust in the trophy cabinet. For example, if you pray in tongues, do so every day. Build it up and try to reach, say, thirty minutes a day. As well as impacting the world by your prayers and enabling God's purposes, it will sharpen your spiritual sight and hearing.

Having the Holy Spirit himself is a gift from God. The Spirit keeps flowing. There is nothing of eternal worth that I can do in my own strength, even with the best of motives. But if I stay connected to Jesus, his promise is that what I do will bless the world. Just as Jesus performed miracles by the power of God's Spirit, that same Spirit is with us today, and is no less able.

#2 The power of God

"You shall receive power when the Holy Spirit comes upon you." [6] What a gift! The Kingdom of God breaks through as a force or power into your life and equips you not only to *be* more like Jesus, but also to *do* more like Jesus. In your prayers you are drawing down from God's vast power station.

As Paul says, God "by means of his power that is at work within us, is able to do so much more than we can ever ask or imagine." [7]

Jesus makes it clear to his followers (that's us!) that he has given them the authority which comes from God, to overcome all the power of the enemy.[8] He does not deny the power of the spiritual forces that come against us, but God is far more powerful and we get to tap into that. The analogy used is of us trampling snakes and scorpions under our feet. We are above them. In our spirit, Paul explains, we are already seated with Christ in heavenly places, far above all the powers of the earth.[9] Everything is beneath his feet so his power can break out anywhere.

I was not in a church or any 'holy place'; I was out in a downtown restaurant having brunch, at the request of a couple I had met the night before. The food was excellent. The light conversation abruptly changed, though, when the man said he wanted me to pray for his shoulder. This was a man who had tried many religions. His shoulder movements had been restricted and painful for several months since a military incident evacuating soldiers in Afghanistan. The place was half-full of customers, but I put my cutlery down, and prayed for healing right there at the restaurant table.

I wasn't sure what God was doing. The first time I checked, there was just a little improvement. Encouraged, I pressed on. Second time: no more progress. Unperturbed, I prayed again. The third time I checked with him, he was lost in disbelief. All the pain had gone and all the movement was back in his shoulders and arms. He repeatedly put them into positions that he hadn't been able to since the accident, repeating out loud, "You cannot be serious. You cannot be serious." I am not sure who he was talking to. I told him that after all that searching for God, Jesus was bringing him home to his heart. The healing was one way of showing him how much he was loved by the Lord Jesus.

The power of God reaches out into even the darkest corners of the earth, where following Jesus is illegal. Christianity is the world's most persecuted religion, and in 2022, the advocacy group 'Open Doors' reported that 360 million Christians were experiencing high levels of persecution and discrimination. Yet God is sustaining them. In North Korea, the dangers of sharing the gospel are immense, but amazingly many are still becoming Christians through supernatural experiences. There is much malnutrition and disease. Christians are helping the sick people by praying for their recovery and seeing miraculous answers. As the Koreans experience the power of God's healing, many are then ready to hear and receive the Gospel.[10] The power of God and the love of God work hand in hand.

God is working powerfully through his family on earth all the time. Rather than fixate on the despairing secularism from your phone's news-feed, look at what God is doing, and pray about things the world will never report on. Then we will see God at work even more.

#3 Prayer and worship

Almost everything we see achieved for the Kingdom is dependent upon prayer. Pray, pray, pray. It is never a waste of time. Yet worship is so interwoven with prayer it is hard to separate them. As you lift up his name, the Spirit comes down. Worship and prayer keep us intimate with God, and give Jesus plenty of chances to interact with us through his Holy Spirit.

At the first New Hope conference, I had emptied myself of everything by the end of the prayer session and collapsed exhausted on a wooden bench. For the second New Hope, after the prayer time I could no longer speak and had a raging sore throat. Having seen all the miraculous healings that year, I was then looking for a chemist shop to buy throat tablets.

But the third year was different. My friend Tracey had come out to lead worship at our third Easter conference in the Gemidgii Stadium. Right from the start I could see there was an anointing on her in Macedonia. During the final two hours reserved for healing prayers, I asked Tracey not to join a prayer team, but to continue worshipping God for the whole time, which was a big ask. The rest of us split up into seven teams.

Jimmy did the rounds after about an hour and a half to see if we were okay. "Are you not overwhelmed?" he asked. I looked at my queue which didn't seem to be getting any shorter, and smiled, saying that I was having fun and could keep going for another four hours. What a contrast. Tracey's worship seemed to energise us, as she sang out songs about God's power and goodness.

Afterwards, Tracey felt that she had missed out on doing the front-line work, by which she meant praying for people and seeing them healed, but you can't underestimate the importance and power of what she was doing. The worship was vital. God was working through her just as much as through those of us praying directly for the people queuing in front of us. That day, we saw many physical ailments healed such as eyes, backs, legs, necks and kidneys. We saw mental anxiety and depression lift from people. One man told me it was his first conference and that he had travelled 150 miles to be there for the day.

Prayer ministry is always challenging. It can be physically and emotionally exhausting. It stretches our faith. That's why God wants to meet us as we worship him, to build us up and bless us as we bless him. Fasting plays an important role too, like turbo-charging the outcomes of our intercession as we give up food or something else for a more focussed period of prayer. If you feel you need to fast for a period, then ask God what type of fast and for how long.

On one trip Jobbo and Tracey had been praying from high places, and singing out worship over difficult towns. The aim was to try to break the powers of darkness over that region and change the spiritual atmosphere. One town that they had been praying for had been particular resistant to the gospel. There was a meal organised by Jimmy there to which guests were invited, but there were others too in the restaurant. Before the talk Tracey sang a worship song to them, during which the presence of the Holy Spirit came and touched everyone in the restaurant, not just our guests. They all applauded and wanted more, so she sang a second worship song.

Four weeks later, Jimmy made a follow-up visit. One of the men in the restaurant wanted to speak with him. He told Jimmy that he had been there on their previous visit, and that day he had been fiercely angry. He had made up his mind to go and shoot and kill someone after he had eaten.

During his meal he heard Tracey sing and it was like no song he had ever heard. It made him feel calm and restful. He then stayed and listened to Jimmy's talk and knew something was speaking into his life. At that moment he made up his mind not to carry out the planned shooting. Four weeks later, he testified that he was still at peace.

#4 The Bible

You can access the Bible every day. It's not complicated to do so. We need to know our Bible. It equips us and grows us. Our spiritual enemy will do anything he can to distract us from doing the right thing, especially engaging with the Bible.

We can't underestimate the Bible's power (though sadly we often do.) One time, I was travelling into the Eastern Mountains that are shared with Bulgaria, to the lovely village of Berovo. Local Christians introduced me to a Muslim man. He had run the local mosque from his home with his wife.

During the food parcel distribution there, they had taken a great interest in the evangelistic messages that had been preached. In the last few weeks, his wife had become fully committed to Jesus, and although he was more cautious his interest was growing. He arrived full of smiles, and I read some Psalms. We discussed how God had always known him, long before he was born. Consequently, when Jesus had been crucified, he could die for my Muslim friend's sins too, because Jesus already knew him. Then I spoke of the value God places on us, quoting from 1 Corinthians. He was enjoying the message and started asking questions, including *"What is this 'Corinthians'?"*

I opened up the New Testament and for the rest of the hour explained how it was all put together. I took him through the Gospels, Acts, the letters from Paul and others, and then talked about John and Revelation. He was like a hot thirsty man enjoying a series of cool beers. I am not sure which of us enjoyed the time most. I felt that fire burning within me as we skipped through the pages. In the months following, my Muslim friend faithfully attended the little local church. The encounter came not a moment too soon for him as six months later he contracted the Covid virus and died.

Get serious about reading the Bible. There never seems to be a limit to what you can find in there. Memorising it is a great tool too. I wish I had learnt more memory verses over the years. My recall of scripture is still quite poor. If your memory is not great then, like me, frequently underline inspiring verses in your Bible, and remember where to find them. In that way, you can use these verses in your prayer times. It really makes a difference. "For the word of God is alive and active. Sharper than any double-edged sword"[11].

#5 The name of Jesus

I had often sung the words of a popular worship song, "There is power in the name of Jesus". I enjoyed singing it, and of course never doubted it was true. Yet at the same time I did not understand how true it was, untilI was at my first New Hope conference, praying for my first person, the lady with the deaf ear. *In the name of Jesus, be healed.* She was. Since then, I have repeatedly witnessed the power that the name of Jesus holds, and I am in awe of it.

Paul wrote to the church in Colossae, that everything you do or say, should be done in the name of the Lord Jesus, as you give thanks to God the Father through him.[12] I always pray now in the name of Jesus. It is an immense weapon to have in your spiritual toolbox.

#6 The blood of Jesus

People don't like speaking about blood. When Christians talk about 'being washed in the blood of the lamb'[13], it does sound weird and disgusting. However, what we are talking about here is what Jesus did for us, when he died on the cross.

In Old Testament days, lambs and goats were sacrificed as offerings to God, in exchange for a worshipper's forgiveness. The blameless and sinless Jesus became the Lamb of God by willingly dying for us, so we could be set free and forgiven. As he died the huge temple curtain miraculously tore in two. It had separated the Holy of Holies (the domain of the High Priest only) from the people. If you accept Jesus, then the divide that had been there between you and God is now gone. When we talk about 'being washed in the blood', it refers to His blood cleaning away all of our sins, and making us able to come into God's presence.

When we pray the 'blood of Jesus' into any situation, we are laying claim to what Jesus has already achieved on the cross. He died to set us free. What the blood touches, the blood cleanses. There is power in the blood to defeat the enemy's plans. *'Lord, set this person free by your blood. Heal this person by your blood.'*

We no longer need a priest. We are free to dwell in the presence of

God, pray for healing, and even perform the duties of a priest (like blessing people), all because of the blood.

#7 Anointing oil

'Christ' is a Greek word from the verb for anointing (smearing) with oil. Jesus is Christ, the anointed one.

The anointing of Old Testament Kings and priests was a specific sacred act done with oil. However, Jesus himself was not anointed by oil, but by the Holy Spirit at his water baptism. We who follow him are similarly anointed by the Holy Spirit. The imagery of anointing in the Bible has water, oil or Spirit bringing about a new or enhanced dimension of spiritual life. Anointing through the Bible symbolises those moments where people or places become bridges or portals between heaven and earth, to receive a special blessing or a new God-given role.

Yet in the early church, we see that even though the early Christians were already anointed by the Holy Spirit they are using oil for anointing some individuals who were sick. We see church elders visiting people, perhaps just those who were very ill and housebound, anointing them with oil and saying a faith prayer for healing[14].

When praying for the sick, I do not normally anoint with oil especially where I have a queue of people, but I still like to have a small container of anointing oil with me. A small shampoo bottle that comes free in hotels, is a good size. I fill it with pure olive oil, pray over it, and close it securely. Then, on particular occasions, usually prompted by the Holy Spirit, out it comes. This could be for healing of a severe illness, or for an anointing to a new calling, such as to a prophetic or healing ministry.

If the person is happy to be anointed, I will pour some oil onto my fingertip. I slowly speak out a few words over them such as, "I anoint you in the name of the Father, Son and Holy Spirit." At the same time, I smear a cross on the person's forehead. In doing this I am inviting heaven to earth, the Spirit to come into and through this person. Come in power, Lord.

For me, at least, it is something I neither completely ignore nor feel obliged to do. Instead, it is there as an optional tool in my spiritual warfare toolbox, to bring out and use as I feel led.

#8 Your testimony

Most people love stories. No matter how short or long you have been following Jesus, you have a testimony, a story of how you became a Christian and what God has done for you in your life. I wish we would share more testimonies in church because they are great encouragement. And your testimony also does something more profound. When the apostle John wrote about the final battle between good and evil, he said that the faithful overcame Satan by the blood of the Lamb and by the word of their testimony[15].

You may not be a great evangelist or preacher, but you do have your unique story. In the Revelation passage, the power of your story is put alongside the power of what Jesus did in dying for us. That takes some processing. Your story really can set people free. It can lead to salvations and healings. Jesus said to his followers that he would make us fish for people[16]. Galilean fishermen used lights to attract the fish at night. Your story can be a powerful and attractive light.

Recently, I had the opportunity to speak to a whole school of about 800 children at an open-air assembly. I simply shared the experience of when I stopped breathing at the age of 11, and what God did for me since then. Then I told them that Jesus was bigger than all their problems. That day, children responded to that testimony and many indicated they had received healing in their bodies, including quite a few with respiratory problems like those I had.

They now had a new testimony of their own.

Work on your story, and carry it around in your back pocket, ready to share. Make sure it's in your toolkit.

#9 Your money and resources

If we're going to work in God's way, we must share his love, often through very practical action. The North Macedonian church has always done this. Early on, staying overnight in their Mission House in Tre Chesmi, I woke up one morning to find a mountain of second-hand clothes piled outside. Pastor Jimmy was there and read my inquiring look. "Part of our humanitarian work," he smiled. Soon a group of people arrived and started sorting through the clothes, selecting what they wanted for themselves. At the same time, two men were bringing out roll after roll of roofing felt from somewhere in the house, and loading it into a small trailer. I didn't ask. The ministry has many aspects.

Accordingly, when Covid-19 struck, the church went into overdrive. Many people in Macedonia could not earn an income and thus could not afford rent or food. The church came up with a food parcel for £15 that would feed a family of five for a month. It was amazing value. It included a 25kg bag of flour, which alone would have cost £40 in the UK. Then there was a separate bag full of the following: 1kg oil, 1kg sugar, 1kg lentils, 1kg beans, 1 packet macaroni, 1 packet noodles, 1kg rice, 1 can fish, bread spread for children and a pack of biscuits (the only luxury item). They also put in Christian literature including a Bible, which was given out with the food; provision for the body and for the soul.

Unsurprisingly, the UK-based Mission Macedonia team got excited about the idea. We could not go out there and minister, but perhaps we could do even more from a distance. We raised enough to fund 1000 food parcels, five times more than we expected.

The first photos back were from the food distribution from the children's church in a desperately poor region. One photo of a man carrying his food parcel, with a huge smile on his face, brought home to us what we were doing. He could now feed his family. What joy! Obeying Jesus' command to feed his sheep opens hearts, challenging the dark social and spiritual forces that keep people impoverished.

When I first got out to North Macedonia during the pandemic, I prayed healing for a man in Kriva Palanka experiencing pain but also a lot of issues with stress and anger. He was anxious because he had no money for his electricity bill and was about to be cut off. I asked Jesus how to pray for this man. To my surprise, Jesus' answer was that this man's financial anxiety could be solved without prayer: I had in my wallet the relatively small amount of money he needed. After we had prayed the peace of God and healing into his body, I found a discrete moment to pass the money over. He was certainly not expecting it and the joy and excitement all over his face was beautiful. Of course, financial gain must never become an expectation of those we pray for, but how many times do we pray for something to occur, when we ourselves already have the means to make it happen? Can my time or my resources be the answer, as well as my prayers?

Maintain the kit

This spiritual toolkit is available to each of us. Take it with you. Know how to use it and be ready to do so. We sharpen these tools by regular use, so don't let them go rusty.

Thank you, Jesus, for giving me everything I need to do everything you ask.

Learning keys

God has given us what that we need to engage with his mission on Earth i.e.:-

The Holy Spirit.
The power of God.
Prayer and worship.
The word of God (Bible).
The name of Jesus.
The blood of Jesus.
Anointing oil.
Our testimony.
Our money and resources.

References

1. Matthew 7:7

2. John 15:5

3. Galatians 5:22-23

4. 1 Corinthians 12:4-11

5. 1 Corinthians 14:1

6. Acts 1:8

7. Ephesians 3:20-21

8. Luke 10:19

9. Ephesians 2:6

10. Open Doors Magazine, March/April 2023 p5

11. Hebrews 4:12

12. Colossians 3:17

13. Revelations 7:14

14. James 5:14-15

15. Revelations 12:11

16. Matthew 4:19

13: The Miracle Of Forgiveness

Asbury College outpouring 2023

It was February 8th. The normal Wednesday morning chapel service at Asbury had finished, but around twenty students lingered in the hall. In a moment of openness, one young man confessed some sins to the group. With that moment of repentance and forgiveness, the atmosphere changed.

Worship continued all day as more and more students trickled in. Something special had started. The worship continued and people kept coming to the altar and saying sorry for what they had done wrong. Repentance led to reconciliation. In other words, as the students pleaded for forgiveness from God, they were empowered to forgive others.

The Bible verse that they had been sharing from Habakkuk was "Look at the nations and watch, and be utterly amazed. For I am going to do something in your days that you would not believe, even if you were told." [1]

Two years of pandemic and its restrictions had hit the Gen Z students hard, but now Jesus was pouring his love into them.

The worship continued non-stop for 12 days. The hall filled with students. Those witnessing it commented on its simplicity. There were no high-tech presentations or charismatic speakers, just low-key worship and an altar to pray at.

As word spread, more arrived from every US state, and then from countries all around the world. Over 50,000 came in the 2 weeks that the service lasted. Overflow venues were set up, but in the end the police could not cope with the volume of traffic nor with visitors camping out around the town. The open service was stopped.

Yet as visitors left, they carried the revival torch back with them.

What characterised this revival was not healings such as in Cwmbran, though these happened. Nor was it people overcome by the Spirit with charismatic manifestations such as at Toronto Vineyard. The focus here was hearts of repentance and on submitting to the word of God. This opened the door for forgiveness to flow. With forgiveness comes release, reconciliation and profound lifelong changes.

In the words of student Khalil, "We've seen people healed. I've seen lots of reconciliation, which has been a really awesome cornerstone of what's going on here. And so I've seen people that have very much not liked each other, and we know this, and then they're praying and dancing and worshipping together." [2]

The miracle of forgiveness is not perhaps as obvious as a physical healing, but the impact on an individual can be even more profound as emotional, relational and spiritual chains are broken. This in turn can be the catalyst for healing of mind and body.

The prison

On a recent trip to East Africa, I was asked to speak in a men's prison. It was an opportunity I had been looking forward to so much. Now, I was pumped. In front of me were over 200 prisoners; some wore the prison's grey stripy uniform, but a third were on remand, wearing their own clothes. They could be in there for months before their hearing. To my left I could see a guard facing me from a wooden watch-out tower. To my right, men sat outside the covered area, leaning against the grimy cell walls and listening from a safe distance. The PA system was loud. Behind me there was a lot of activity in the courtyard. Some were completely ignoring what was going on but others listened whilst trying to look disinterested. I tried to engage as many as I could from each direction.

After I introduced myself, I felt compelled to start by sharing one of my favourite stories.[3]

"After the end of Apartheid in South Africa, a Truth and Reconciliation Commission was set up. During one hearing, in the presence of the victim's mother, a policeman named van de Broek recounted how he had shot an eighteen-year-old boy and burned the body on a fire to destroy all evidence. Eight years later he returned to the same house and seized the boy's father. The wife watched as her husband was tied up, had petrol poured over him, and was then set alight. The courtroom became completely silent as the judge offered the widow the opportunity to respond. "What do you want from Mr van de Broek?" he asked.

She asked van de Broek to go out and collect the dust from the place where he had burned her son's body, so she could honour him with a proper burial. He was so ashamed he could not look her in the eye, but nodded in agreement. Then she added, "Mr van de Broek took all my family away from me, and I still have a lot of love to give. Twice a month, I would like for him to come to my ghetto and spend the day with me so that I can be a mother to him. I would like Mr van de Broek to know that he is forgiven by God, and that I forgive him too. I would like to embrace him, so he can know my forgiveness is real."

As the elderly woman pronounced those astounding grace-filled words and walked towards him, some in the court started singing an old hymn."

I looked over the sea of prisoners, and started singing the first lines of that hymn:

> *"Amazing Grace, how sweet the sound,*
> *That saved a wretch like me..."*

Van de Broek, I explained, did not hear the singing because he he had fainted, overwhelmed by the widow's forgiveness.

Those who were listening that day in the prison were deeply moved; some trusted the rest of their lives to Christ that day. We prayed for dozens to be healed. I knelt in the dirt with one man, Amos (a 40 year-old on a life sentence), as he wept loudly and declared later to me that he wanted to be an ambassador for Christ.

Unknown to me, two of the burly men standing in the prison yard under the hot African sun were a former pastor and his brother-in-law, who had committed a murder over a property dispute. Resenting the man who had come to help find a resolution, they had ruthlessly murdered him. He was the brother of their local bishop.

After my talk, the two men were so convicted by God that they pressed forward asking us to pray for them. It was the first time they had shown any remorse in prison, but now the Holy Spirit had spoken to them so clearly, they wanted the bishop to come to the prison as soon as possible, so they could ask him for his forgiveness. The absence of bitterness brings freedom. They accepted they may never leave the physical prison, but now they had the means to break out of the prison of bitterness that their minds had been locked in. It is called forgiveness.

'Where the Spirit of the Lord is, there is freedom'.[4]

How many times should I forgive?

The disciple Peter asked Jesus, "Lord, how many times will my brother sin against me and I forgive him and let it go? Up to seven times?"[5]

The cultural expectation at the time of Jesus was similar to today. If you owe me, or have done me wrong, then you pay. Against this background, Jesus has brought his radical message of grace and forgiveness. Peter had been with Jesus nearly three years, and he got it. You must forgive people.

When a Rabbi made a judgement after much debate with his disciples, then they had to live by that rule for the rest of their lives. One Jewish Rabbi had taught that you should forgive three times but not a fourth time. So Peter is looking to Jesus (his Rabbi or Teacher) for a rule to live by. *Seven is the perfect number, so would that make a good upper limit for our forgiveness, or is that going too far, Jesus?*

Jesus however comes back with an answer which would have surprised everyone. Not seven times, but seventy times seven. In other words, no matter how many times somebody wrongs you, you must forgive them. Whatever they have done to you, you must forgive them.

Peter already saw that forgiveness is really important, but Jesus takes us to a different level entirely. Following Jesus means that forgiveness must become a lifestyle. You must live a life of forgiving grace.

And that level of forgiveness is not natural. It requires a miracle in us. The Holy Spirit has to come in and do some serious rearranging of our emotions, our thoughts, and our personalities.

From the cross

The forgiveness of God is in itself supernatural. Jesus died for us on the cross, so that we could be forgiven and made acceptable to God; this is the miracle that most impacts our lives. Let the power of confession and forgiveness transform you and your ministry. It needs to become a daily habit. That's why Jesus placed it as the climax of the prayer he taught his disciples: *Forgive us our sins as we forgive those who sin against us.*

If we do not embrace that forgiveness and apply it to others who have hurt us, then we smother our happiness and our progress as a Christian. And if your unforgiveness is inflicting damage on others and yourself, how can God perform miracles through you?

This miraculous gift of forgiveness is the reason the South African mother was able to forgive van der Broek, despite the extreme pain and grief he had inflicted. The Holy Spirit was now giving the same life-changing gift to these two murderers in the African prison.

Learning keys

The grace of God and forgiveness is a miracle that can set you free and allow you to set others free. It can release the power of the Holy Spirit in you.

There is no limit on how much we must forgive, but it is God that gives us the strength to do it.

Unforgiveness is a barrier to seeing all that God can do in you and through you.

References

1. Habakkuk 1:5

2. Fox News Flash, Feb 22 2023 11.00am

3. Simon Guillebaud, Choose Life 365, (Oxford: Monarch Books 2014)

4. 2 Corinthians 3:17

5. Matthew 18:21-22

14: Creation Miracles

Water

Two of the three boreholes had been successful. Yet in this third remote landscape, where the Church had already started a medical clinic and a new congregation, it had all gone wrong.

The survey had predicted water, but the borehole didn't find it. The drill then hit some unexpected rock and got stuck. The hole was now capped off with a welded plate. The rains had not come and the whole area was like a dust-bowl. Without the borehole it was a long and uncertain trek to get water.

How would you pray in this situation?

The most obvious is to pray for rain. We did that. I had checked my weather app. It was going to be a steady 31C (88F) all day. No rain. None predicted for the next 10 days either. Two hours later as we were leaving, the temperature unexpectedly dropped a few degrees, a wind blew up, the blue sky was quickly replaced by grey clouds and it started raining lightly. As we drove away towards our base, the rain got heavier. It was nowhere near what they needed, but it was an encouraging sign that God was with us.

A second prayer was needed. If the borehole did not find the water, perhaps we could pray that the water would find the borehole. Of course, this would require a miracle, what we call a creation miracle. I thought of how badly the local people felt about their borehole failing. They might be tempted to ask *Why us? Does God not like us?* Then I thought of how they would feel if God did a miracle and brought water to their barren bore hole. *Wow, why us? We must be really loved by God.* I could not get the prayer out of my mind.

One of our team had wandered down to the borehole on the first day and said she could hear something. The next day when we returned, a larger group of us went there to pray again for the miracle and to investigate. There was a noise of air rushing out of a smallish gap below the welded cap. When you put your hand by it, you could feel this strong, steady flow of air. Where was it coming from? It seemed plausible that water had indeed found its way into an underground cavern and was displacing air which was then being forced up the borehole. Could our prayers be being answered? Could water have already found its way there? As our time in Africa progressed, we heard from the pastor that the steady stream of air was continuing and its noise and intensity had increased. This continued after our return and belief was strong back in Africa that the water would soon be springing out.

Shortly after we returned to the UK, the initial prayer for rain was fully answered. For the first time in three years, there was three weeks of hard rain, restoring the land and filling all the water tanks to overflowing. Phenomenal!

A long time ago, Moses and Aaron were in a similarly dry place. God had led them to a rock in the wilderness and they had a large assembly of the Israelites with them. Moses lifted his hand and struck the rock twice with his staff. A large flow of water gushed from the rock. Everyone, and all their livestock, drank from it.[1]

Jesus was in Jerusalem at the Feast of the Tabernacles. Every morning during this joyful feast, a priest would take a golden vessel to the Pool of Siloam, fill it with water from the pool and take it to the altar amongst the chanting of Psalms from the crowd. However, on the eighth and final day of the feast, the ritual was not repeated, and that was the day Jesus chose to make the shocking statement that he was the rock from which the living water flowed. What he had to offer us was the real deal and not just the waters drawn from the local spring.

"'Let anyone who is thirsty come to me and drink. Whoever believes in me, rivers of living water will flow from within them."[2]

Whilst we pray for much-needed physical water, we should not overlook thirsty people who also need the life-giving Holy Spirit.

Weather

Sometimes you do not want the rain.

The long-range forecast for our third New Hope Easter trip had been for sun every day, except for the Saturday when rain and thunder were anticipated. This was the one and only day where we didn't want any rain, as it was the day of our open air 'Big Grill' evangelistic event. I had not been too worried, as forecasts always change nearer the time. Except this one didn't.

On the Saturday at our morning prayer meeting in the mission house, I checked the weather app. Thunder and heavy rain from midday. We all prayed that the rain would hold off until the end of the event. It was an early start, and gloriously sunny as we set out, all wearing our bright yellow 'New Hope' T-shirts.

In Gradsko town centre, there is a performance area with steps arranged like a mini-amphitheatre, the perfect location for our open air 'Big Grill'. Some of the Macedonian team had a resource stall, and others were grilling food. Large grilled sausages in a wrap proved especially tasty; Macedonians love grilled meat. We had performances from 5 music groups (from Wales, England, Croatia, Bulgaria and Macedonia). There were preaching slots from three of us, leading into salvation appeals and ministry times.

With a very successful event under our belts, we quickly packed everything away by 2.30pm, at which time the first spots of rain fell. We had made it and were now safe in the vans. As we pulled away, thunder boomed and a torrential downpour began. Incredible timing. Four years later the same thing happened. With rain forecast all day, it rained heavily up to the start of our event in Gradsko, was sunny during the event, then after the clear-up it rained so hard that the roads became rivers. That same year, as we were doing some open-air worship, we watched as the wind pushed a huge grey rain cloud in our direction. We prayed for the rain to stay off; the cloud stayed motionless for an hour even though the wind blew throughout that time.

Of course, the sceptics will always claim that what we see as an act of God is just pure coincidence, and perhaps sometimes it is. Many weather prayers are said, and I guess most make no difference to the weather pattern. However, that does not mean we should never pray for the weather, especially when the outcome will have significant impact on the work we are doing for God. That day, we really needed the rains to hold off and they did for the exact time we needed.

When Jesus was once awoken in a boat, he found his disciples fearing for their lives, as a storm lashed over them. He stood up, gave the winds a telling off, and then commanded the waves to settle down. They did. All became calm.[3] Hardly a coincidence.

Vehicles

Perhaps we don't talk about it, but I suspect everybody at some time or other prays for their vehicle.

On one occasion when I was a teenager, I was invited to a party in some remote rural location, along with a friend. I persuaded my Dad to trust me to drive his car for the evening. All went well until the car stuttered to a halt in the middle of nowhere. It was very dark. I didn't know what to do. Mobile phones had not yet been invented. Fortunately, further down the road I found a cottage with a light on. A man came out and looked at my friend and me in our ridiculous party gear standing there, grinning in the light rain. A moment later he was striding down the lane to look at the car, wielding a powerful torch. It turned out that he was a car mechanic. He told me I needed a replacement alternator for my

Dad's MG1300. I had no idea what he was talking about. He said that (amazingly) he had one in his shed that would do, and there on the spot he fitted it. We had no money. He shook his head, and told us to go straight home. We gave the party a miss.

A few years later, I was driving back from Llanelli, where I had been helping out on an information weekend for the missionary group, World Horizons. It was a dark, wet night. My old Austin Maxi was well known for its poor condition, a car which seemed to regularly spray oil onto the underside of the bonnet. As I drove across the Severn Bridge that joins Wales to England, I realised I was in trouble. The engine was rapidly losing power and it was all I could do to coax it off the motorway into the service station at the end of the bridge. Where could I get help? Mobile phones had still not been invented. I prayed. When I did, an RAC rescue van appeared near me. It had been sent out to help another car. I stood by the mechanic in my raincoat and prayed quietly as he mended the other car. Then I asked him if he could help me. He said he would but then remembered to ask me if I was a member of the RAC. I wasn't but told him that I was just about to join. I got home safely that night and joined the RAC the next day.

I always make sure I have plenty of petrol in the tank, but have heard of many stories from Christians who seem to have driven many long miles without any fuel. On one trip to Macedonia, I felt the Spirit telling me to stay on there for another three days and follow his voice. This was new for me. Jimmy was gracious, and gave me both a car and a young driver for the duration.

Our journey took us through the mountains of the remote Marovo National Park, 300 square miles of wilderness and beauty. For no particular reason, I glanced down at the fuel gauge: the tank was empty, or about to be. I pointed it out to Darko, and said he had better pray that there was a garage just around the corner. The Park is sparsely populated; we had been travelling for a long time and not seen a single petrol station. Almost as I stopped speaking, we rounded a corner and on our right was a petrol station – the only one in the whole range.

Food

As a young man, I trekked across the Kabyl mountains with my friend Jono and another lad. Having accidentally lost most of our money in a taxi dispute, we were now far more reliant on God to survive. Amazingly, when we entered a remote village, people would come out with food for us. On my birthday, a local resident (who did not know the occasion) brought us a whole roast chicken, bread, figs and a bottle of wine.

One day, however, we were particularly thirsty and hungry. We had not found a village, but there was a derelict place by the side of the road that we could use for shelter from the wind. We decided to spend the night there.

At the centre of the ruined hamlet stood an old well, but we had nothing to draw the water. We prayed. Shortly after, a boy drove up on a moped with a bucket. He drew his own water and then drew more for us, filling our water-roll and bottles. No-one else came, and a mist descended as the sun dropped below the horizon. It was getting cold so we pulled our sleeping bags up around us. Then through the mist we saw a man coming towards us. Where had he come from? He walked right up to us, gave us some bread rolls, and then left without saying a word. We thanked him and gratefully ate our simple meal. We commented that there must be a homestead nearby; surely he had seen us walk past his house earlier. The next morning, we woke to a very clear sky and could see for miles: there were no homes to be seen anywhere at all.

The stories of Rolland and Heidi Baker, missionaries in Mozambique, have been a great source of inspiration and encouragement to me. On one occasion, they had no food and had not eaten for several days. Their baby daughter Chrystalen was crying from hunger. Someone from the US embassy called at their door with a meal for them, enough rice and chilli for all four. Heidi smiled, and explained that she had an unusually large family. She opened the door fully to reveal all the additional street children that they had taken in, sitting along every wall of their main room. The embassy worker was aghast; there was no way that his meagre contribution could feed everyone. But Heidi encouraged him to pray for the food he *had* provided. A hundred people were well fed that day from a meal intended for just four.[4]

This account is strikingly similar to an Old Testament story where during a time of famine a man brought 20 small barley loaves to Elisha at his school of prophets. He instructed his servant to serve them up to the 100 students. Everyone ate and there were leftovers when all had been fed well.[5]

Better known, of course, is the occasion when Jesus takes the little boy's gift of 5 bread rolls and 2 small fish, gives thanks to God for it, and then feeds the 5000 Jews. There are 12 handbaskets of leftovers collected.[6] Later in a remote place in the Gentile (non-Jewish) Decapolis, Jesus scouts round his disciples for the little food they have left and blesses the seven bread rolls, and few small fish. He gives thanks to God and feeds the 4000 Gentiles until their stomachs were bloated. There were seven large double-handed baskets of leftovers.[7]

Blessing the insufficient

When God provides, his provision is abundant. If he chooses, he can provide far more for each of us than we could possibly need. The wedding of Cana was another example of this super-abundance of God, as Jesus turned the water in 6 large stone jars into red wine.[8] The servants who are the least "important" people at the feast, can only provide water. The insignificant offer the insufficient. But Jesus speaks and the miracle happens. Jesus provides the equivalent of maybe seven extra bottles of the finest wine for every guest at the wedding, far more than they could possibly have needed.

In our hour of need, we the insignificant (in the eyes of the world) bring the little we have to Jesus and ask him to bless it. We make ourselves available and give our time, our money and our resources, as we are able. Where we come up short in his service, we can pray to be blessed by his abundance.

Why not?

These are just a few of my own small stories of God's provision when in a tight corner, as well as others I've read about. Those who do not have eyes of faith will underline that word 'coincidence' again. It is an easy option. Yet why shouldn't God trump nature's rules now and again to provide for his children?

In the time of Jesus, men over 20 were expected to pay an annual temple tax (probably equivalent to about 2 days' wages, traditionally referred to as the 'two-drachma tax'. Peter was discussing this with Jesus, who pointed out that kings did not tax their own families, and implied he was exempt from any tax required for God's work. He was family! However, so as not to offend the tax collectors, he told Peter to go to the sea and cast a hook and take the first fish that came up. *Open its mouth,* promised Jesus, *and you will find a four-drachma coin. Take it and give it to them for my tax and yours.*[9]

Whilst creation miracles may or may not be hard for you to believe in, pray for them anyway, whenever you are in that place of real need, or see others that are. He is the great provider.

Learning keys

First, do what you can yourself, such as maintaining your vehicle and putting fuel in it. However, when you are in need of a creation miracle, pray for it.

When you are in need, God can provide through others and even through angels.

God gives superabundantly. He can take our little and multiply it if he wishes too.

Be creative in your prayers. Can your ministry opportunity or obstacle be solved by a creation miracle?

References

1. Numbers 20:10-11

2. John 7:37-38

3. Mark 4:39

4. Craig S Keener, Miracles Today (Grand Rapids: Baker Academic 2021), 181

5. 2 Kings 4:42-44

6. Mark 6:31-44

7. Mark 8:1-9

8. John 2:1-11

9. Matthew 17:24–27

15: Raising The Dead

Was I or wasn't I?

Looking back again on the day that the 11 year-old me stopped breathing, the natural instinct is to say that I did not die. Perhaps after I collapsed, I somehow started breathing again and revived fully within the next 30 minutes or so? What did actually happen to me?

There is a clear explanation for why I *stopped* breathing. As the wet paint dried in my room, the volatile organic compounds (VOCs) from the solvent-based paint evaporated into the air. As I lay in my bed, I inhaled them and, as I was asthmatic and susceptible, they inflamed and swelled the inside walls of my lungs. The airways narrowed until I could no longer breathe, which is when I woke up briefly before collapsing.

After all these years, I still have not found a simple natural explanation for how I *started* breathing again. How did my airways recover to the extent that I felt fine, and not even mildly asthmatic in that moment? The VOCs had not dissipated, as they can actually stay in a room for up to 6 months. I took no helpful medicine or inhalers in that period. The only reason I can come up with is a supernatural one. While I guess I will never know all the details of that night, I am left convinced that God answered my mother's prayers and brought me back, giving me a second chance to live.

That said, my own level of expectation about the power of prayer to raise the dead has always been low. Apart from my own story, I have never seen it happen, nor have I ever expected to see someone raised from the dead. I like hearing the stories of what resurrection miracles Jesus performed, but can we really follow in those footsteps?

When the American speaker Robby Dawkins came to our church, he said that he was praying for resurrections whenever he got the chance, but he was still waiting to see one. I remember cynically thinking, *Well, good luck with that mate!* On a subsequent visit, however, Robby reported his then recent experience of a man that stopped breathing in one of his own meetings in a church near Preston, England. The man had appeared to be clinically dead. Dawkins prayed for him and the man started breathing again and then recovered.

I still have not myself witnessed someone being raised from death, but Dawkins' account raises my faith a little, as do the stories I share below. They help me to pray the bigger prayers.

The Jellyfish Man

In current times no less than in the Biblical era, people have resurrection stories that are both fascinating and entertaining. Perhaps none more than former atheist Ian McCormack who had been night diving in Australia and swam into some highly poisonous box jellyfish. He was stung five times on his arm. He finally got to a hospital but paralysis was leading to death.

His Christian mother, on the other side of the world, saw an image of her son and heard God saying that Ian was at that moment close to death and she must pray for him now. In the ambulance, Ian saw his life flash before him. Then in his mind saw his mother praying for him; she was saying, *Ian, call out to God from your heart. He will forgive you, Ian.* As he lay in the ambulance, he saw words from the Lord's Prayer appear in lights before him which he then made his own. He surrendered his life to Jesus and was filled with peace.

The ambulance doors opened. They raced him into hospital but by now he was in 'crash mode'. He could move nothing but his eyelids. He lost his pulse, then the monitor on his vital organs flat-lined. He was clinically dead. As his blood was poisoned by neuro-toxins, he was pronounced brain-dead. He was moved to the morgue.

What followed was an out of body experience in which he witnessed first hell then heaven. Meeting Jesus, he was asked if he wished to stay. He could think of no reason to go back to his body, until he had a clear vision of his mother. For her alone, to show her that her prayers were affective, he opted to go back. Then in a split second he opened an eye. A doctor with a scalpel was pricking the base of his foot as he lay on a slab in the morgue. The doctor jumped out of his skin, and the nurses in the room fled.

Ian was later told that he had been dead 15 to 20 minutes and no medical interventions had been undertaken to bring him back. Waves of God's power flooded through him over the next four hours until he was completely healed. He walked out of the hospital believing in the resurrection power of Jesus Christ. Ian has then spent the next 40 years plus going around the world telling everyone his story.

In the final stages of editing this book, I checked directly with Ian that he was happy for me to relate his experience. My thanks to him for his (very prompt and very gracious) agreement.

In Ian's testimony, I am particularly struck, by the power of his mother's prayers. It reminds me of my own mother. Mums, don't stop praying for your kids.

An expectation that we try

Is bringing people back from the dead really expected of us? Surely not? Even to contemplate praying for a dead person surely seems ridiculous? Jesus himself raised some dead people to life, but can he really have expected his followers to do the same?

Apparently so. When he sent out his disciples in pairs on their mission trips, he told them what to do with their time.[1]

> *Preach that the Kingdom of Heaven has come near.*
> *Heal the sick.*
> *Raise the dead.*
> *Cleanse those that have leprosy.*
> *Drive out demons.*

Okay, but that was the 12 chosen ones. Could this expectation not have been for them alone? Well, clearly not, as we see evidence of resurrections in the early church too.

In Joppa a disciple named Tabitha, full of good works and acts of charity, became ill and died, and when they had washed her they laid her in an upper room, Peter was urged to come over. When he did, he turned out the mourners and said to the body, "Tabitha, get up." She opened her eyes, and seeing Peter she sat up.[2]

Later, during one of Paul's lengthy talks, a young man, Eutychus, falls asleep, and tumbles out of a third storey window. He is found dead. Paul takes him up in his arms, prays for him, and his life returns.[3]

So it continued. One hundred years later, Iraneus, a church father, claimed that the dead were often raised through the prayers and fasting of true Christians. 200 years after that, St. Augustine of Hippo and other church leaders of the time reported eye-witness accounts of resurrections. Throughout the medieval period and into modern history there has been no shortage of resurrection claims.[4] The case of Ian McCormack (the "jelly-fish man") is just one in a long line of such miracles going back to Jesus.

Muamba

In 2012, I was enjoying a televised FA cup match, Bolton Wanderers away at Tottenham Hotspur. In the first half, we were all horrified as midfielder Fabrice Muamba, just 23 years old, suffered a cardiac arrest on the pitch. In the stadium watching the match was leading cardiologist Dr. Andrew Deaner. He ran onto the pitch to assist.

When the heart stops, the blood supply to the brain stops. Cells begin to die off after 3 minutes; you would expect the patient to be brain dead after about 20 minutes. Eventually after 78 minutes, the medics got his heart beating again. Muamba was rushed to the specialist coronary care unit at the London Chest Hospital. A press campaign was started to 'Pray for Muamba' and many around the world began to pray for Fabrice's recovery. Footballers wore 'Pray for Muamba' t-shirts underneath their kits. Churches up and down the country held prayer meetings for the young man.

About two weeks after the incident, Muamba regained consciousness. He had no brain damage. Dr Andrew Deaner told the BBC: "If you're ever going to use the term miraculous, it could be used here." Muamba later said, "I thank God because I am alive. Without him I would surely be dead. This is a miracle; the power of Jesus Christ has raised me up and I thank everyone for their prayers and support throughout the world." [5]

Death in the pool

I think back now to when I had been invited to do the mission in Mombasa, the bustling port city on Kenya's east coast. I spent the days in the motel preparing for the evening meetings.

On my last day in Mombasa, as I was eating breakfast, I head a cry of alarm; staff were running towards the swimming pool. By the time I got there a lady had been dragged from the deep end. She was lying motionless in the recovery position with a small crowd around her. I went over. She looked dead. I stood near her and prayed in tongues. When challenged, I said I was a pastor[6] and was praying. That was accepted.

After about 10 minutes or so, thank God, she came round and was able to stand up. Later she explained: *I'm a swimmer and I'd actually been in the shallow end. But then I felt something drag me under, and drag me into the deep end.*

Since I'd arrived, I'd swum in the pool every day; there were no vents or drains in the pool that could have done that. Maybe she had just panicked but that seems unlikely. I suspect it was a case of witchcraft, a reality that beyond doubt many in Africa face regularly. I don't know the signs well enough to be sure, but it was certainly a mysterious event. I don't know what difference my prayers made, but I was glad I prayed.

Praying for resurrections

I do not for one minute think that I can add anything useful from my own experience on how to pray for the dead. If I were praying over a loved one, I would spend some time pleading with God, and might try commanding the death to go and life to return. My level of faith would probably be low, but in the moment a surge of faith is possible, as happened to me when praying for the young man with the face tumour and for blind Beti.

Among various accounts I have read, the one that spoke to me most was of Dr Sean George who died of a heart attack in 2008. His medical friends tried relentlessly to bring him back, long after they should have given up. By the time his wife reached the clinic, he had been dead for 1 hour 25 minutes and his body was cold. He also had suffered acute kidney and liver failure. Instead of going in and saying her goodbyes, she took him by the hand and offered a simple prayer for God to give them more time together.

"Sean is just 39, I am just 38 and we have a 10 year-old boy. I need a miracle."

Immediately his heart starting beating again. He gradually made a full recovery and within 3 months Sean was back working full time. He kept all the medical records to prove the miracle to the sceptics.[7]

If you ever find yourself in that situation, pray for a resurrection miracle with whatever words come to mind, no matter how ridiculous it feels, or how low your faith is. Try anyway.

Learning keys

Jesus expected his followers to pray for the dead, to see them raised to life.

People have been brought back from death with some regularity since the time of Jesus.

Whilst it may seem to you extremely unlikely, do not discount the possibility that Jesus could bring back to life one of your loved ones. You need to pray.

References

1. Matthew 10:7-8

2. Acts 9:36-42

3. Acts 20:7-12

4. Craig S Keener, Miracles Today (Grand Rapids: Baker Academic 2021) Part 5

5. New Life Publishing, May 29th, 2016.

6. Christian workers in Kenya are generically described as pastors

7. Craig S Keener, Miracles Today (Grand Rapids: Baker Academic 2021), 163

16: Why Are Some People Not Healed?

It is right to pray for healing?

There is no suffering and sickness in heaven. When we pray the Lord's Prayer, we ask for his kingdom to come, and his will to be done on earth as it is in heaven. I believe these words from Jesus give me permission to pray health, instead of sickness, believing that this is God's best for anyone that requests it.

The Bible records that Jesus not only spread the Good News and did many miracles, but he also sent out his disciples in twos to do the same, first the 12, but then a wider group of 72 followers. Later, as Luke takes the story into the book of Acts, we see the early church doing the same. Why would any less be expected of us?

It is actually very hard to come up with a convincing argument from the Bible which says that the modern-day followers of Jesus should *not* be doing the same as the disciples and early church. There is nothing in the New Testament that in any way implies that the first disciples' way of praying for healing would not apply to successive generations of believers, including us. As crazy as it seems, we have been given the power and authority to do what Jesus did. When Jesus said to his followers that they should expect to do greater things that he did[1], I think he was actually telling the truth.

Why are some people not healed?

But there's an elephant in the room, isn't there? Let's just ask the question straight out. *Why are some people not healed?*

It was 1996, and Cross Rhythms festival dance venue was packed and pulsating with teenage energy. White wings attached to the arms of our dancers shone brightly under the UV lights, as I shouted, "See your hands in the air." Dance music was the craze. S'dANCE was a Christian dance worship outfit; I had helped produce their album, which we were now gigging. I was high on adrenalin as we launched into our album's title track, *And the angels raved on*. Yet only half way through our opener the stage manager grabbed me: *"Shut the music off!"* he implored. A man at the front had collapsed. His heart was beating too slowly for him to be safely moved. Could someone say a prayer urgently?

A tense hush descended in the tent as I led everyone in a prayer for healing. The words just came to me as I opened my mouth. Afterwards I looked down to the paramedic and got the thumbs up. The heart beat was back to normal and he could now be taken to hospital. A cheer rose and we launched back into the set. The festival-goer spent the night under observation and then was back on-site next day, perfectly well. It felt like God really had sent his angels to party with us that night.

Before the gig, a quirky young man had found his way back stage and started praying for me. The Holy Spirit's power that quickly came on me was not only palpable – it was immense. It rooted me to the spot; I was standing up but couldn't move. I was there for some time but though I was electrified by the experience, I eventually had to pray, *God please release me, I need to get on-stage and do the gig*. Fortunately, God did.

Much later as the spotlights went out and the tent spilled its human contents back into the camp-site, I went back-stage again. *Will you pray for me?* someone asked, *For my back?* Another person asked if I'd pray for a painful knee. I had never done this before. I agreed though, and to my surprise each told me their pain had gone after I'd prayed

Then... *Would you go and see a girl in a caravan with a local group of young people?* someone else asked. *She's suffering badly from asthma and wants you to pray.* I was still asthmatic myself, so that wasn't going to happen. It was now gone 1 a.m. I made a feeble excuse and didn't go. Next day, I heard the girl had got worse and been taken to hospital. I felt guilty. When she was back on site, I went to the caravan to apologise. Whilst there, I said a simple prayer for her that she would be healed of asthma, then left. But that was it; I thought nothing more of it.

I had my first asthma attack when I was very small. I was told that having been left with a babysitter, I got really upset and the trauma brought on the asthma. At times in my life, my condition has been quite severe; I know what it is like to struggle to breathe. *Wouldn't it be so good if I could be healed once and for all,* I've said to myself. But it has never happened.

A few months after Cross Rhythms, S'dANCE were doing a gig at Kingsbridge in South Devon and we were delighted when the group from the caravan turned up. The girl I'd prayed for was there.

"How's the asthma?" I asked.

She looked back at me surprised: "What do you mean?"

I replied that I remembered her being very ill with asthma at the festival, so I wanted to know how it was now.

She laughed, "Don't you remember? You prayed for me for it to be healed. I haven't had any asthma since."

I could not have been more shocked.

I somehow concluded that the miracle healings that I saw at Cross Rhythms as a young married man were a one-off, linked to that Holy Spirit anointing before the gig. It was nearly twenty years before I prayed for sick people again.

After all, *why was she healed of asthma, and not me?*

I'm sure that you will have asked God a whole range of questions about healing prayer. Here are just some that I've heard or asked myself.

- Will I give this person false hope, if I pray for them? Aren't I just making things worst for them mentally, when I pray for them and they are not healed?
- Some churches say that God doesn't heal people supernaturally today. Maybe they're right? How do I know?
- If we have an illness or disability ourselves, we can empathise with others. There are high profile Christians whose disabilities give a platform to inspire others. People like Joni Eareckson Tada, the famous Christian author and speaker who was paralyzed from the shoulders down at 17 after a diving accident. Or Nick Vujicic, the Christian evangelist and motivational speaker born without any arms and legs. *Are some illness and disability intended by God? If they are, should I be praying healing prayers at all?*
- Why is it I can pray for nearly two hours for the healing of so many at a New Hope conference in Macedonia, see so many miracles, and then end up with a sore throat afterwards?
- And above all, why are some people healed and not others?

As I have prayed and studied the Bible over the years, a number of things have helped me understand this, to some extent at least. Let's spend the rest of the chapter on them.

#1 The place of faith

Faith is defined in the Bible as "confidence in what we hope for, and assurance about what we do not see." [2] The spiritual battle that we are in isn't something we can see with our eyes. Nor can we see the power available to us through the Holy Spirit. We just know from our Bibles that they are there.

So, how much faith do you need to see a miracle?

Q1: If I am sick, is there something wrong with my faith? No. God does a lot of healing, in different ways, but sometimes we stay sick for a short or long duration. Though the sickness did not come from God, we need to be open during that time of ill-health to anything He wants to teach us. In the introduction to his popular devotional *Choose Life,*[3] Simon Guillebaud tells of how he was at the peak of fitness when fatigue hit him hard for many months. He decided that, whatever the root cause of his sickness, he would not let Satan have the victory in this and indulge in self-pity. Living within his new set of restrictions, he decided to write a devotional book from his sick-bed. It is a book that has impacted many lives. He chose life over death, within his illness. We can have sickness in our own bodies, but still be walking by faith in the power of God.

Q2. Does the person you are praying for need to believe in Jesus? Do they then need to have a strong enough level of faith in Jesus to believe in their own healing? The gospel accounts of miracles are interesting in this respect.

A lady suffering non-stop menstrual bleeding for twelve years fights her way through a crowd and touches the hem of the Rabbi's cloak.[4] Jesus sees the women and tells her to go in peace because her faith has made her well. Another time Jesus commends a centurion for his great faith and immediately heals his servant from a distance.[5] Yet there is not an inkling of faith to be seen anywhere when Jesus heals a paralysed man at the pool of Bethesda,[6] or the man born blind begging at the gates of Jerusalem.[7] Neither even asked for their healing.

From my personal experience and from what I read across the gospels, I would say faith in Jesus and his power to heal today is not a mandatory pre-requisite to receive a healing, although I think it helps a lot. Faith seems to improve the odds. When people press forward for prayer at our New Hope conferences or after services in our local church, they often have a high expectation that Jesus will heal them.

Q3: *What about the faith of the person praying for the healing?* Do I need to believe that God will answer my prayer or can I still pray whilst racked with doubt? My own example praying for the asthmatic girl at Cross Rhythms festival would suggest that God can step in when you are obedient but your faith is low. Many other people give similar testimonies to mine. So I would say it is not necessary, but it is really helpful to have that confident belief that the Holy Spirit can work through you and do the healing. I believe now that a good level of faith increases the likelihood of you seeing positive results.

Q4: *How do I get that confident belief?* Faith is not something you can easily talk yourself into or manufacture on the spot. However, you can train yourself over time to increase your faith levels. If you or I hear of, or read of, miracles happening today, it can help us to believe that we can see miracles for ourselves. That is the main purpose of this book. But if you are actually present and you witness someone being healed, your faith can strengthen even more. That's why we bring less experienced people out on trips to Macedonia, so they see for themselves what the Holy Spirit does. Best of all, though, is to give it a go yourself and see God heal someone as you pray. You'll need to step out and, yes, risk failure in order to get there. When you do that, your focus should not be on how big your faith is, but on how big your God is, in whom you have put that faith.

If you are connected to Jesus, the vine[8], don't fear going out on a limb for him; that is where you will find the fruit.

#2 The role of experience

As you pray more often for people to be healed, you learn not to rush into a formulaic prayer. It's vital to listen to God. Otherwise, you can miss something really important. Listening does improve with experience.

When we pray for healing, we are engaging in a spiritual battle for the health or life of that person. Lack of experience might mean we have missed an issue that needs sorting before our prayers can be effective. The person may still have an undisclosed pack of tarot cards at home, or unforgiveness in their heart, or a trauma that the mind has blocked out, or a sinful addiction that they are not facing up to. These can be barriers to the healing. If we do not discern them and deal with them, we are unlikely to see the breakthrough.

Alternatively, we may not have the right tools or experience yet for a certain battle. At that moment, this may be a miracle which is outside of our spiritual reach. We may need more practice at smaller battles first. Maybe start by praying for headaches, body aches and pains with some lack of mobility. I don't know of anyone yet that started their prayer ministry by going up to someone in a wheelchair and seeing their leg grow back. That said, in the spiritual sense, God is still in the business of taking down giants like Goliath, using small boys like David.[9] So it is possible.

Healing prayer seems to require a lot of listening to God, and his promptings can be hard to pick up on. It takes practice, and it's always best to work with and learn from others.

#3 The impact of culture

Is it easier to see miracles happen in some countries than others? Do the cultural differences in Macedonia and Kenya impact people's readiness to see miracles? The short answer is: *Yes*.

For many in Macedonia, poverty, sickness, abuse, and loss of close family through migration, is all too common. When offered good news of hope, food, or prayers to be healed of sickness, the chances are they'll grab it. Often, they desperately want to believe and are happy to come forward even at the risk of nothing happening.

In Kenya, there are churches everywhere, though faith in some places, as they say, may be "miles wide but inches deep". The occult is everywhere too and can cause great fear. As a result, God, miracles and demonic activity are all part of normal life. It is both hard and unwise to be agnostic there. Charms and curses bring highly visible dangers, so if you are not to be destroyed by evil, the power of God to protect and heal is an absolute necessity.

In richer countries, we have good access to medical help, so we naturally look to the doctors for treatment more than we look to God for a miracle. As Christians we should give thanks to God for enabling us to learn about the human body and medicine, for the breakthroughs and for the wonderful trained staff who can apply these remedies and practices. We should give thanks to God whether we are healed by medicine, or by miracles. He designed the nature that holds the healing properties, and the science that leads to our surgical procedures being successful. When we pray for healings, we should be as open to a medical solution as to a miracle one. The way our human bodies are designed to self-heal is also God's gift.

Western affluence, however, brings the illusion of self-sufficiency. So let's pray for a hunger in our communities that will see people throwing themselves at the feet of our benevolent God. And for compassion and courage in ourselves and in our churches, so we'll take God's love and power to the people we live alongside. For our neighbours' sake, go against the flow of society's downstream pull. Mental illnesses, isolation and relationship breakdown are growing rapidly. With this backdrop, more people are starting to realise that more medicine is not the solution, and are starting to look to God for an answer.

#4 Signs

The New Testament frequently uses the term *sign* rather than *miracle.* God often does dramatic miracles to get people's attention, especially during outreach into a new area that may have to date been resistant to him. This is one reason why you may see more miracles when you are working in cultures that have for a long time opposed the faith. Such power encounters may be purposeful signs from God to demonstrate that he is greater than the power of the local religious influencers, such as witchdoctors.

Once some religious leaders turned up and demanded a sign, a miracle from Jesus. They were not willing to accept the many things he had already done; they wanted more. Jesus refused them.[10] Signs and miracles come from God's goodness to us, not from any obligation that we may try to place on him. We cannot pressure God by unwarranted scepticism or by demands for something "different". The world revolves around him, not us.

Miracles were never meant to be the answer to all of the world's problems. They are not an excuse for us to do nothing. They are a foretaste of a better future, where we live continuously in the love of God. They show us how much God cares about our health and how we should care about it too.

If you developed Type 2 diabetes through overeating, it would be great if you were healed by someone's prayer. However, it would be even greater if someone had taken you under their wing earlier on, and at the first signs of you putting on weight, had lovingly helped you and supported you in adopting and maintaining a healthy diet.

If there are fewer obvious signs or miracles in one place than in another, it does not mean that God is not at work. It just means that he is working in different ways.

#5 There's a war going on

The Bible tells us that the Kingdom of God is both here and is to come. The 'now' and the 'not yet'. The Bible speaks of an age to come when Jesus returns and God's kingdom and reign of power will be fully established on Earth. There will be no more pain and suffering, but the chance for people to repent will also have gone.

We are clearly not there yet; the Bible says we are in a battle.[11] Nevertheless, God intervenes supernaturally far more now than in pre-Jesus days. Why? Because the future kingdom of God started to break through when Jesus came to earth, and has continued to do so ever since.

In this war, God has chosen to partner with us! It means that whilst God remains all powerful, our earnest prayer "releases" our God to move in that power. He waits to release his power until we pray. We see a good example of this in the book of Acts, where the apostle James has been put to the sword by King Herod, and because the king saw this had pleased the Jews, he has now arrested Peter. The apostle is heavily guarded in prison. Many fellow believers in Jesus are locked into a prayer battle in the house of Mark's mother. It sounds like they were going at it for many hours, as they interceded for Peter's release. Then finally the breakthrough comes and an angel appears in his cell in the darkest part of the night. He wakes up Peter and guides him out, as the iron prison gate miraculously opens by itself. Prayers have been answered, and Peter is free.[12] War always involves waiting. Victory is never instant. In the Bible, we see lots of examples of conflict situations, some being resolved just two days later. Why not the next day? Jesus is crucified on the Friday and is resurrected on the Sunday. In the Old Testament we see Abraham willing to sacrifice Isaac, and two days later an angel offers up a ram in the place of his only son[13]. Esther prayed and fasted to prevent a genocide of her people, and on the third day approached the king and won his favour, enabling her plan to save the Jews suceed[14]. As we have already seen, Jesus is victorious right now but we still have to await the complete experience of his victory. Whether two days, weeks, months or years, we may have to wait for the prayer to be answered. Don't be disheartened. Don't give up.

Why does God delay until his children pray? Because he wants them to see miracles. And through those miracles, they will see him.

Is the Holy Spirit going to heal every person that you and I pray for every time? No. It's a battle, and God is asking us to join in, be persistent and patient if needed.

#6 The wilderness

When Jesus said he had come to bring you life in all its fullness,[15] he did not mean that he would take you seamlessly from one exciting event to another. Most people who have spent a long time on the Christian walk will be familiar with the 'wilderness'. It is a period of life that can bring you prolonged loneliness, need, fatigue, worry or suffering. Sickness and pain are often a part of it. Experiencing Jesus as a close and personal best friend may only become a true reality to you for the first time in that place. You plunge yourself into more prayer and develop more reliance on the Holy Spirit's strength to bring you through each day, as you dig deeper into the well of God's resources. They are times not of judgment on you, but provision for you.

Jesus often went to a wilderness place to pray, to get renewed strength for his ministry. For us, the wilderness places can be like a spiritual gym. They enlarge our soul and equip us to come out the other side, stronger and fitter in our faith.

In our ministry for others, out of the compassion we have for them, we want to spare them from any ordeal, anguish and heartache. We try to fast-forward them out of it through our prayers. Yet it may not be God's priority for that person at that time; he may in fact be allowing the physical suffering in order to encourage improved mental or spiritual health. The term in the Bible that is closest to our word "health" is *Shalom,* but it includes so much more richness and depth. It's about being restored to the person we were always meant to be, in right relationship with God, with others, with our mind, our body, our spirit.

The apostle Paul suffered from a persistent illness or disability. Whatever it was (we don't know), it was severe enough for him to call it a "thorn in the flesh". In Paul's own words: "Three times I pleaded with the Lord to take it away from me. But he said to me, 'My grace is sufficient for you, for my power is made perfect in weakness.'"[16] Physical healing, God was explaining, was not what Paul needed most. Even the resurrected body of Jesus had not been healed of its physical scars from the crucifixion.[17]

In the West especially, we tend to see health as the absence of illness, generally physical illness. But God wants to give us so much more. Without his inner healing and forgiveness, we're in a sort of war with ourselves, with others and above all with him. Jesus offers us peace and wholeness (Shalom) instead of war. That absolutely extends to our body, our mind, our relationships, our identity. But the order in which they are healed is up to him.

There is a warning here not to demand physical healing from God as some sort of entitlement. If a prayer for physical healing is not answered straight away, it may be that it is not top of God's priority list for that person. At such times, we should expect our prayers to go unanswered.

It is also important to remember that healing miracles themselves to do not lead people to faith in Jesus. Those without faith still need to know the Good News of Jesus Christ and make that decision to follow him. Sooner or later, each of us will die. At that moment what will matter is not how healthy we have been but whether we have welcomed Jesus as our Saviour. When you pray for someone's healing, whether you see results or not, don't leave the job half done: help bring them into the saving light too.

#7 Embracing failure

Faith, experience, culture, signs, waiting and the battle for the 'not yet kingdom' are all helpful windows into unanswered prayer, but surely they cannot be the whole picture. To me there is still a big element of mystery about what God does and what God does not do. I will always have questions about 'what went wrong this time'. I am happy, though, for my faith to embrace both doubt and mystery. *Lord, I do believe; help me overcome my unbelief.*[18]

When you write up your testimonies, it brings the highlights sharply into focus, particularly those events that amazed you and that you hope will encourage others. Yet, there is so much more in the mix including the hard work, disappointments, financial cost, heartache and, of course, the non-healings. These are often closely intertwined with the miraculous.

Disappointment in Mombasa

On the fourth evening of my mission trip in Mombasa, I pointed out that all who had come forward at our services for prayer that week, had received their healing. I encouraged them to put the word around and to bring more sick people to the services.

Next day when I arrived, there was a group of five young men in their early twenties who had travelled 50km to be there. A few years previously one of them had been carrying one end of a very heavy wooden beam on his head, the weight shared with a friend at the other end. The friend had stumbled and dropped the beam. The beam's full weight fell onto the first lad, crushing him and breaking his spinal cord. His four faithful friends had brought the paralysed lad to the service to be healed.

Not knowing what would transpire, I had already planned to preach that day on Jesus healing a paralysed man who had been lowered through a roof by the four friends that had brought him. I would emphasise the faith of those friends. Expectancy was high in the church. I had asked for more sick people and had got my wish. But I had never prayed for anyone who was in such a bad state as this young man. Did I have the faith to do this?

Whilst the church worshipped, I went to pray for the young man but there was no improvement. I left him with the pastors praying for him, whilst I prayed for others that wanted prayer, then returned for another go. I was told his spinal cord was damaged all the way up into his brain. I held his deformed hand as I prayed, but felt no response in any part of his body. In the heat he was sweating, his eyes rolling, and I could see a tear drop from his left cheek.

Prophetic pictures sometimes appear in my mind, and on this day I "saw" little lightning flashes going up and down his spine. Surely this was the Lord starting to make better nerve connections in his back, the start of a recovery? Yet there was no change observable at all. I shared the picture with them, but then could only apologise that the healing we had all hoped for had not happened. That evening I agonised over it and was left with a lot of questions.

But by the next day, I realised God was asking me a question. It's a question that you also need to face if you commit to praying for healing with others: *Are you willing to take disappointment and pain on board from those that are not healed, if that is the price for seeing others restored to health, wholeness and blessing?*

It was a pivotal moment for me. *Yes,* I told God, *that is a price I'll pay.*

Perceived failures have two effects on me. First, they fuel my doubts the next time I pray. Will God really use me again to bless this next person in this new situation? I start to worry that I may have lost an anointing. But they also make me more resolved to push through the doubt, to try again and to ask for more.

We are storming the darkness with the light of Jesus, reclaiming what is rightfully his. It is a challenge where we are not guaranteed success. But our persistence goes a long way.

As Paul assures us: "We also glory in our sufferings, because we know that suffering produces perseverance; perseverance, character; and character, hope. And hope does not put us to shame, because God's love has been poured out into our hearts through the Holy Spirit, who has been given to us." [19]

The incomplete picture

An individual photo in a wedding album does not adequately describe the day. The whole album gives you a much better insight but is still not the same as having been there. Similarly, the parables of Jesus give you numerous different insights into the kingdom of God but don't reveal its fullness.

The arguments given above, when combined, will hopefully give you some appreciation of why your prayers are not always answered. However, in that moment when you pray for someone to be healed and they are not, there will still be a degree of mystery surrounding that unanswered prayer.

We should push forward in the understanding that we will never fully grasp '*the why*'. We should rejoice in the miracles we see, whether they happen quickly or over a long period, and hold very lightly to the disappointment of those we don't see answers to.

Learning keys

There are many reasons why a prayer may not be answered in the way you want, and when you want. Don't let it put you off persisting in prayer.

Sometimes the prayer will be answered, but you need to wait for it.

Push forward in your gifting. Be grateful for what you have achieved in Jesus, rather than bemoaning what you haven't.

Building your faith up is important, but God can still do miracles even where there is lack of faith or expectancy either in the one praying, or the one being prayed for. He is bigger.

You are work in progress, and always will be until you meet Jesus face to face.

Do not expect miracles to be the answer every time. God works in many ways.

References

1. John 14:12

2. Hebrews 11:1

3. Simon Guillebaud, Choose Life 365, (Oxford: Monarch Books 2014)

4. Matthew 9:20-22

5. Matthew 8:5-13

6. John 5:1-15

7. John 9

8. John 15:1-17

9. 1 Samuel 17

10. Matthew 12:38-39

11. e.g. Ephesians 6:10-11, 1 Peter 5:8-9 etc

12. Acts 12:1-11

13. Genesis 22:1-14

14. Esther Chapters 5 to 7

15. John 10:10

16. 2 Corinthians 12:8-9

17. John 20: 24-27

18. Mark 9:24

19. Romans 5:3-5

17: Storming The Darkness

Make no mistake, if you accept God's invitation into his miraculous work, you are entering a war zone. The Bible spells it out for us as we read about the New Testament church. In Macedonia or in much of Africa, that spiritual warfare is likely to be obvious. In wealthy parts of Europe or North America, it may be much more hidden but it's just as real.

We need to ask God to open our eyes to the spiritual reality *wherever we are.* If you want to see miracles, ask the Holy Spirit to open your eyes to the urgent struggle that is going on just below the surface in your street or your workplace, among your friends and even your family.

The deaf dumb boy

On the surface, all looked fairly normal. A deaf dumb boy was brought to the front of the church. He was calm. Then the moment we started praying for him, he went berserk, punching and trying to stamp on our feet. He had to be restrained. Jimmy had said this would happen. It was the demon in him reacting to our prayers.

The state of the deaf dumb boy remained unchanged as he returned home with his parents; we knew from experience that this would take more prayer than we could offer that day. The demonic spirit in him was strong and would fight hard to stay. We cannot physically see the forces we are up against in the spiritual realm, so we are fighting blindfolded to some extent. Some do have a gift of seeing directly into the spiritual realm, but for most of us, the only understanding we get is guidance from the Holy Spirit. That experience certainly brought into focus the underlying spiritual war that is so often hidden in the West.

"We fix our eyes not on what is seen, but on what is unseen, since what is seen is temporary, but what is unseen is eternal," says Paul [1]. "Our struggle is not against flesh and blood, but against the rulers, against the authorities, against the powers of this dark world and against the spiritual forces of evil in the heavenly realms." [2]

Paul tells the church in Ephesus that Christ has been raised into the heavenly realms, above all rulers, authorities and powers [3] (these include the demonic). He is the source of all our victories and breakthroughs. All things are under his feet, and the power that raised Christ to that position is the same power that is working in us. We should hate the works of darkness, and know how to operate in the authority and power that Jesus has given us over it[4].

This book alone cannot equip you for a deliverance ministry. You will need further help and study if that is where you are led. However, we all need to be aware of this other spiritual dimension. My advice is to not go looking for demonic trouble, but sometimes it is unavoidable, or you are the only one who can help in a given situation. To overcome the enemy, you need to take that authority given you, plug into the Holy Spirit's voice and leading, and use your prayers and the scriptures to do the fighting.

The man with the tumour

Where does the illness come from? Is it always demonic? Most times, no, it isn't. As the deaf-dumb boy sat down with his parents, a large man came forward for prayer, He had travelled to Veles from another town, and had already received prayer once to no avail. He was in a serious condition, because doctors had identified a tumour in his head. It wasn't visible to us. This time, there did not seem to be a trauma or anything demonic behind it, so we simply commanded the tumour to go in the name of Jesus. My faith that God would act was not strong. Even when your faith is faltering, you should still give it your best shot in prayer and see what happens. After all, as we have already seen, the victory is not dependent upon our faith levels.

A few weeks later, Jimmy rang me to say that the man at the service had returned to the doctors, and the tumour had gone. In its place was a fairly harmless cist. Wow! Most illnesses are not be caused by demonic activity but they are still part of a broken, fallen world; they are not what God wants.

This chapter, however, is about recognising and overcoming the dark spiritual forces that lurk beneath the surface more often than we realise. God is the victor, and he gives us strength and protection to storm the darkness. Let's have a look at two more encouraging examples of this.

The haunted house

"Let's burn the blanket." the cry went up.

"Yes, burn it."

The blanket was whipped away from my gloved hands. A young Roma man produced a lighter and before I knew it the blanket was ablaze in the middle of the balcony, watched with approval by a circle of Macedonian men. That was not what I was expected to see on Easter Sunday.

The day had started as we set up the Gemidgii sports stadium in Veles, where the third New Hope Easter Conference was being held. This town in the centre of North Macedonia is the ministry hub for the church network, though at that stage their rented building was far too small. The ministry needed a new home where more could be done. That day, Jimmy had promised he had a treat in store for us; together we would inspect what was locally called the "Haunted House."

Jimmy had found this impressive four-storey building with a balcony that overlooked the river Vardar and offered beautiful vistas up to the surrounding mountains. Internally it was in a terrible condition, but structurally it was fine. The man who owned it was in Germany and had given up trying to rent it out because it had a reputation of being haunted. No-one could last for more than a month or two there, so it had become un-rentable and had fallen into disrepair. Its reputation also made it hard to sell.

Our Mission Macedonia team started dreaming with Jimmy about helping him raise the money to buy the haunted house, kick out the spirits and develop the property. It had such potential to be something amazing for Jesus, with training facilities and accommodation as well as a base for the growing Veles church. Lots of prayer followed. Now we were back, and the sale of the property was going through at a very low price. Time had now come for the evil spiritual residents to move on.

A large team drawn from the UK and Macedonian young leaders moved through each room in turn, worshipping and praying. I was handed a small book by John Eckhardt entitled *Prayers that Rout Demons*[5] and was told which sections of the book to shout out and declare at each point of the house. "I break and release the house from all curses of death and destruction in the name of Jesus." (One of our team, Pastor Katrina had considerable experience of deliverance, having spent much time ministering in Africa. The trouble was that she'd lost her voice on the trip, so I became her wingman to shout and declare deliverance scriptures over the house as directed by her. I had not done this before but have a loud voice, so eagerly undertook the role.) Perhaps surprisingly, there were no demonic manifestations. One lady felt that the dark spiritual occupants had just decided to go and find somewhere else, when they came across so many of us intent on routing them.

Katrina had discerned that there had been a baby or toddler killed in the house, because it was deformed and was not wanted. She was unaware that this was one of many babies born deformed as a result of soil pollution from the nearby smelting factory.

A picture had come into Katrina's mind of a blanket that had been used in the sacrifice. After praying for guidance, we looked for it and actually found the blanket at the back of the patio behind the house. This was where the murder had taken place, we sensed. Once the Macedonian lads had seized it, the blanket was up in flames within a minute.

In one room, we found lots of toddlers' shoes which had been left behind and we disposed of those. Another team member, though, sensed we had still missed something. Whatever it was, he felt that it was hidden in the loft, so we checked up there with a torch. There was just one item in it, tucked away in a far corner. It was a baby bath, perhaps also used for the terrible deed and then hidden away to help cover over the guilt.

It was a tragic affair that had brought such evil into the house, but we felt good that after many years we had at last stormed the darkness and helped release the building's potential for God. Returning to the balcony we enjoyed the warm sunshine and spectacular views. *This balcony is so spacious,* I commented, *we could fit 200 people on it, no problem.*

As we watched from the balcony, a wind started blowing; it was carrying a cloud of seeds, suspended delicately in the air. New Life. New Hope.

Life hanging on a thread

I first got to know Adams, Pastor Jimmy's son, in the small village of Crveni Bregovi (Macedonian for Red Coast, due to the soil colour). It is where Adams and his wife Maria run their church meetings. We often referred to it as the Children's Church as children made up most of the congregation. The mosque in the same village had started bribing the children not to go to the church. *Come to the mosque instead,* they said, *and we will buy you a bicycle.* It was a false promise, but it seemed plausible, and half the children left.

One day early in 2022 Adams suddenly collapsed, and had bleeding on the brain. He fell on his 2 year-old son, who screamed out. The screams were heard by his wife Maria who immediately called for medical help. He was taking initially to a local hospital with few facilities, whilst he was prepared for a transfer to the main hospital in the capital. Meanwhile everyone prayed. The situation was critical.

From the start we prayed for Adams intensely. His brain haemorrhage, we felt, was a spiritual attack on a key young leader. Indeed it, was part of a much bigger spiritual battle against the ministry team in Macedonia, and also against the churches and the country itself. Yet we were confident in our God of miracles.

Adams was able to undergo an emergency operation to stabilise him, stop the bleeding from the aneurism and do some immediate repairs. However, this was only a temporary measure; his life was still in the balance. A second much more complex operation was vital. There was no one in the whole of North Macedonia that could do it. One surgeon in neighbouring Serbia did have the skills, but would he be able to travel to Macedonia?

Back in the UK, our Mission Macedonia team embarked on a prayer vigil for Adams, with daily zoom meetings for prayer. We put the word out and more and more people got engaged in prayer warfare for Adams. The request on our Mission Facebook page got 2000 engagements, far more than our posts had ever had before. An online church held a week of prayer and fasting.

There was a two week wait for the Serbian surgeon and then, at short notice, he delayed a further week. All the time Adams lay in critical condition in a Skopje hospital.

As we pushed in with our prayers, we started feeling attacks on ourselves and our families too. For me, it was a particularly tough few weeks. My father, Albert, lost his seven-year battle against dementia and died. I returned from my mother's home both emotionally and physically drained, and took one of the standard Covid tests. I tested positive. Persistent tiredness dogged me for six weeks after I'd shaken off the Covid. Had the ME viral fatigue that I'd endured for seven years during my thirties, now returned? I managed my days carefully, fighting such thoughts, and kept praying for Adams throughout.

When the surgeon finally arrived from Serbia after a nervous three weeks' wait, it was a long and difficult brain operation. He completed 70% of what was needed long-term, and decided that he had done as much as he safely could that day. Adams was now off the danger list. He would live. Praise God.

Nevertheless, our prayer was for a 100% recovery in God's timing, and we truly believed that we had won that position in prayer. We also believed that God would continue the healing in his brain even whilst he rested. Adams was allowed home to his family. On his next check-up, they decided that his brain was healing and they would delay the rest of the surgery.

During my prayer times I got a picture of Adams looking well and sharing his testimony of God's goodness to him at a New Hope conference.

A few weeks later, I stood on the Veles HQ balcony with over 200 others, kick-starting New Hope after the enforced two year lay-off. Tears in my eyes, I watched Adams share the testimony of his healing. He explained that he had felt the presence of God with him at all times during his illness. Even in the darkest hour he'd never been afraid. It was a wonderful and powerful moment for all the churches to hear him share his personal experience of God's goodness and miraculous healing.

A few months after the conference, he finally got the operation on the last 30% of his brain and made the full recovery we had all interceded for.

Put your hand into the hand of God

It is late 1939: the Second World War threatens to sweep everything of value away. King George VI struggles to know what he can broadcast to a worried and fearful nation. Princess Elizabeth (the future Queen), then just 13, hands him a poem by Minnie Louise Haskins. It has been stirring and strengthening the hearts of millions ever since.

> *And I said to the man who stood at the gate of the year:*
> *"Give me a light that I may tread safely into the unknown."*
> *And he replied: "Go out into the darkness and put your hand into the Hand of God.*
> *That shall be to you better than light and safer than a known way."*[6]

Following Jesus is a narrow path[7] that leads into the darkness. He's not calling us to huddle in our well-lit churches ignoring the suffering outside. He wants us to storm the darkness. Every time you put yourself forward to pray for someone's healing, you are storming that darkness.

Will she be saved? Will he be healed? Am I going to see a miracle today? We hope so but we don't know, nor do we need to know it. What we do need to know is that King Jesus, the King of Kings is the way forward. He is the truth, he is where life is found [8], and he will never leave us. [9]

God wins

And the rewards of storming the darkness are enormous:

"The blind receive sight, the lame walk... the deaf hear... and the good news is proclaimed to the poor." [10]

The new church HQ building in Veles is a visible demonstration of God's power. That day, when for the first time the balcony was full for New Hope 2022, many were saved, blessed and healed. Miracles were happening in front of our eyes. Just as they had happened when the Apostle Paul first visited Macedonia. Just as they are happening around God's world today.

When we were praying for Veles, we had a picture of a lighthouse growing up through the ground at Veles and breaking through the hard rock, shining light all around the county. Where the light fell, there would be spiritual warfare and God would win.

Wherever we live, we can learn to storm the darkness, and see God's miracles. To do that, we need to be willing to get on the front line. Just below the surface, there's a spiritual battle going on. You can't win it alone. You need the Holy Spirit and you need his church around you.

Are you ready with a heart of love, to step out onto that front line, to help Jesus win in each situation, as his hands and feet, as his ambassador, as his prayer warrior?

Yes.

Good, then Jesus says, *Step out with me.*

Learning keys

If you accept God's invitation into his miraculous work, you're entering a war zone. It may be hidden but it's real.

The battle is the Lord's. But we need to get involved; if we don't get involved in his war, we won't see his victories.

Be careful in deliverance situations. Listen to God before jumping in. Do not go looking for 'demonic trouble', but prepare yourself, as best you can, for when you are led into that type of spiritual conflict.

References

1. 2 Corinthians 4:18

2. Ephesians 6:12

3. Ephesians 1:20-22

4. e.g. Matthew 10:8, James 4:7 etc

5. John Eckhardt, Prayers that Rout Demons (Charisma House, 2014)

6. 'God Knows': first published in Minnie Louise Haskins: The Desert (Privately printed, London 1912)

7. Matthew 7:14

8. John 14:6

9. Matthew 28:20

10. Luke 7:22

18: Over To You

'It's gone, it's gone.' That moment of shock, awe and then joy at New Hope 2018 when I realised the Holy Spirit had healed the young man of his face tumour, still inspires me to push on for more. Indeed, I've been inspired by so many of these experiences that I have shared.

Did I understand everything I witnessed? I think not. I suspect there were times when I thought God had done something in someone's life when he hadn't, or had done something different. There would be many more times when, as a result of our prayers, God did miraculous things that we never got to see or hear about. That said, what I have shared with you is definitely how I recall it. I have tried not to exaggerate or sell it short. In most cases it was first written down or recorded within hours of it happening.

This is not the book to take anyone into some premier league of elite world-renowned 'Holy Spirit-filled mighty warrior-healers for Christ'. I do hope, though, that my testimonies encourage you to make yourself available for the team sheet, then get out onto the pitch and play. Come and join me in the lower leagues. Give it a go, even if you are rather late to the party (just like I was).

We all need to start somewhere. At some point a young schoolboy picks up a javelin for the first time and throws it just a few yards. He has to start somewhere on his quest to become the Olympic athlete who will win gold for his country. We should never despise small beginnings. Celebrate each step forward, no matter how small you perceive the miracle.

A guide to healing prayer

How, though, do you actually go about praying for someone for healing? Let's look at some basics.

Jesus prayed for healing in all sorts of ways. He did not leave us with a formula, which I find reassuring. He was dependent on God for power and direction and so are we. But there are some elements which are usually in place when I pray for others. It is the way I do it, and I am sure others will approach it differently, but I think it will give you a helpful starting point.

- I do not think it matters where you pray for someone, as long as you are able to focus on God and they have a chance of relaxing and receiving from him in that environment.

- Ask the person's name first and make an effort to remember it before moving on. Many times, I have had to ask for a name more than twice which is not good.

- What does the person want Jesus to do for him or her? Is it a naturally occurring illness such as from an accident, or is there something unusual about it, which could signify some demonic activity? If the sickness is long term, was it linked to a trauma in their past? Try to find out.

- If there is a physical pain, ask them to gauge it on a scale of 1 (barely noticeable) to 10 (very painful). If there is a lack of movement anywhere or some restrictions, then see what can physically be done right now, and what cannot be done. This is your reference point. It will help you later to see what God has been doing.

- Ask the person to close their eyes and relax and not to pray out loud whilst being prayed for. It is you that is doing the praying, not them. Some Christians find it very difficult to keep quiet, but it is important that they just relax and receive.

- Ask for their hands to be held out in 'receive mode'. Explain it as them waiting to receive a gift from God. Don't force it though. Posture helps but it is no big deal.

- Pause. Ask God quietly, not out loud, for some insights, and listen to see if any relevant thoughts come to you. Is there any bad stuff you need to know about, such as unconfessed sin or unforgiveness that could be a blockage to the healing? If there is, then gently ask about it and pray for that first. You yourself may even feel a short-lived pain in the same area that they have pain. Let that encourage you in what God is revealing. Are there any positive attributes about them that God is showing you, that you can encourage them with? If so, start there. It will help them understand that God sees them and loves them. You are ready to pray.

- Typically, to start with I will either place one hand on a shoulder, or alternatively one on the forehead and one on the back depending on what I am praying for. Go with what you think seems right. I make actual contact and 'don't hover' but keep the touch fairly light. Do not apply force and never try and push someone over 'in the Spirit', which is manipulative and entirely wrong. Don't be weird and have one hand high in the air as if you are conducting electricity, or blow on their face. Being prayed for is strange enough for most people, without making it unnecessarily freaky.

- Always affirm the person, then ask the Holy Spirit to come and bless. Wait, and simply ask for *more, Lord*. Try and sense the presence of God at work. This may be a sign you experience, such as your own hands warming up, or you may get words or pictures to confirm what God is doing. It may be signs experienced by the person you're praying for, such as eye-lids fluttering, or body swaying etc. If they are troubled, always ask for the Peace of God to come on them. I often do that anyway.

- For those who are experiencing strange feelings and have not been prayed for before, then explain what is happening e.g.

God is blessing you and what you feel is the Holy Spirit working in you to make things better.

- If there is sickness in the body, then when you feel the time is right, speak directly to the sickness and tell it to go. Pray the blood of Jesus over the person and the sickness. Command it to go in the name of Jesus. Both the blood and the name of Jesus are powerful weapons. Really powerful. Incredibly powerful. Pray to cut off traumas and afflictions with the sword of the Spirit. If you are praying for a Christian, then you can tell the sickness that it has no authority to be in that child of God and must go now. Pray God's health into the body to replace the sickness. If you know your scriptures well, then use them in prayer. Wait a little.

- If I am praying for, say, a leg or foot, then after a while I may get down and place a hand on the afflicted area, especially if it was not healed the first time I prayed. Be very sensitive to where you place your hands. As a guide, anything other than placing a hand on a shoulder may need permission. Never touch private parts, whatever the gender. You may choose to pray for somewhere such as the heart or stomach by getting them to place their hand on it, and then putting your hand on top of theirs. Always be sensitive to the culture you are in and do not do anything that is inappropriate. It is better to be over-cautious.

- Wait a bit more; keep listening to what God might be saying. Don't be pressurised by the silence to rush back in too quickly. Allow time for the Holy Spirit to minister. Some people suggest at this point that, in your head, you go away and make a cup of tea. Then when the time is right, check in. *How are you feeling now? Is there a change? Be honest, has the pain level reduced, and if so, what is it now?* Make sure they are not just telling you what they think you want to hear.

- Is there a partial healing? Where you are already aware of pain levels and restricted movements you can actually gauge the improvement. For anything else, you are reliant on what they feel physically happening (e.g. *"my stomach has warmed up and feels less tight"*), and on any words you yourself have had from God about the healing. In some cases, there may be no instant visible evidence of the physical healing.

- Spend some time thanking God for any healing that you either know or sense has happened. If there is partial healing, even if just a small amount, then pray again as I think more healing is now likely.

- If the person is fully healed after one to three attempts, then thank Jesus again and say a prayer to seal the healing so the ailment won't come back. Be aware, it may still do. If there is partial or no healing, I might leave it after three attempts. Other times, though, I might keep pressing in if I felt that was right. God sometimes heals the next day or later, especially where a healing has begun.

- Remember it is all Jesus, not you. Be excited about the healing, but stay humble and give Jesus all the glory. Always. As Paul put it succinctly to the Corinthians," Our competence comes from God".[1] It is always his power, not ours.

- Remember that God's priority is for spiritual healing over physical healing, so if the person does not know Jesus personally, this would be a good time to give them the opportunity and to pray for their salvation.

- If there is no healing, when you feel you have done your best, then say you are going to leave it there. Thank the person for coming for prayer and send them away with a blessing over their life and their family. Remember again, it is all Jesus, not you. It may not be his will at this moment for that person to be healed, or there may be other reasons. Do not beat yourself up, nor make them feel guilty or responsible for "failing to be healed". Well done for giving it a go.

- Reflect later on how it went and what you may have done better, so that you can keep learning and improving.

- If you are having success in praying for healing, then can I encourage you to pass your experience on to others? And share with others what God has done. It is the Lord's testimony too, not just yours to hide away.

You can't put it into words

Recently, I was on a prayer retreat in West Wales and as always met some wonderful people. One lady, Lesia[2], saw me several times in passing but never spoke to me. On the day I was leaving, I had put some things back in the car and was returning to my room one last time.

Lesia was in the corridor and stopped me. "Are you a healer?" Not a question I had been asked before. She looked a little nervous. I smiled at her. She tried again: "Do you pray and heal people?"

I gently said, "Well, Jesus does the healing not me, but yes, I do pray and ask Jesus to heal people."

She told me that every time she had seen me, she had heard the word 'healing' in her head and was prompted by God to approach me and ask me to pray for her. She had never plucked up enough courage before now to do so. I asked her how much longer she was staying for. She said that she was leaving right now. She had left it until the last possible moment. God gave her this final chance. She had come a long way to West Wales to get some specific blessing or healing from God and had almost missed it.

The little chapel wasn't free, so I asked her where she wanted me to pray for her. She immediately suggested we should walk by the pond as she found it really peaceful there. I asked her what she wanted Jesus to do for her. She indicated that she had a number of things wrong with her, and made some vague murmurs. She clearly felt that she did not need to tell me too much. Some people want prayer from you but expect you to ask God for what is needed, rather than telling you themselves. That is harder but okay. In Lesia's case God had told her that I would pray for her and she would receive her healing. So she was keen for me just to get on with it, which I did.

Whilst praying for her, I discerned a problem in her stomach and intestines, linked to a traumatic event. I said so and she nodded affirmatively but was not going to divulge details. I got her to imagine Jesus physically with her in that traumatic situation back in her past, then prayed for the Holy Spirit to break off the trauma. I then prayed for both her stomach region and for God's peace to fill her mind. I could sense the Holy Spirit at work in her, blessing her and healing her tummy. When I thought we were done, I checked in with her. "Lesia, what are you feeling now?"

She looked up to me, her face radiant with joy, and she just smiled. I tried again.

"What is the change?"

She had clearly been overcome by the Spirit and had experienced God afresh in a way she had not done so before. She had also got the healing she had come for. Again, she smiled and just said one thing.

"You can't put it into words."

Stepping out in faith

How many times does each one of us miss out on a blessing from God because we don't pause to ask what he wants for us to do. Our fear of the unknown or fear of embarrassment can so easily stop us. That was what Lesia had repeatedly struggled with. Although she had heard God's voice several times and listened to him, she was fearful to act on what she had heard. Thankfully, even though it was at the very last minute, Lesia did act and the Holy Spirit was able to bless her as he had wanted to all along. For my part, I had made myself available to God and was there for her when she needed me,

There is a risk involved whenever you act on God's instructions to you, but it is worth the risk every time. If you misheard God or went forward and nothing happened, then what have you really lost? You might look or sound a little silly, that is all. For the potential gains of getting a gift from God, the risk of looking a little silly now and again is a small price to pay.

If you have not yet decided to accept Jesus into your life, then I fully commend him to you. Don't put it off any longer. Find a believer who can explain this decision to you and pray with you, to take that step in becoming a Christian. Only then can you pray for others to see these miracles we have talked about. The good news, though, is that when you are following Jesus, you can start straight away.

I hope the book has helped and inspired you. I also hope that you are motivated to take more risks for Jesus, and see both more miracles and more failures for yourself. Always remember that without the Holy Spirit your ministry is nothing. Without him you are floored.

Next time your friend says she is suffering from a migraine, ask if you can pray for her then and there. If she feeds back afterwards that it does actually feel a bit better now, give thanks to God. Then in that small beginning, get a scent of the possibility that there are greater victories to come. Enjoy the miracles when they do come. And as you see miracles, always remember to give the glory to Jesus.

Your onward journey into the miraculous awaits you. Go for it.

Learning keys

There is no formula for healing prayer. Jesus did it various ways. However, the guidelines given here and by others should help you develop in your ministry.

We all need to start somewhere. Start right now from exactly where you are.

Pray now for your first or your next opportunity to see miracles.

Reference

1. 2 Corinthians 3:4-6

2. Name changed

PART 3
THE EXTRAS

Appendix I: North Macedonia – A Visitor's Guide

North Macedonia is a land-locked country the size of Wales. After World War Two, the region spent nearly fifty years under communist rule and religious groups were harassed to varying degrees. When the communist dictator General Tito died in 1980, Yugoslavia descended into a series of civil wars from which emerged the six independent nations of Serbia, Croatia, Slovenia, Montenegro, Bosnia & Herzegovina and Macedonia.

Macedonia was spared the worst of the conflicts and declared itself an independent state in 1991. Some older people still regard General Tito as a hero and fondly remember those communist days of near-full employment. One communist inheritance is the 'Brutalist architecture' of chunky and angular concrete designs for some public buildings, such as the Gemidgii stadium in Veles where we held our early New Hope conferences.

The renaming of the country as North Macedonia came in 2019, as an accommodation with the Greeks who also have a region named Macedonia. For decades, Greece had used its veto to prevent Macedonia joining NATO and the EU.

This often-overlooked country is 80 per cent mountainous. It has its own language and is probably the most ethnically diverse country in Europe. The Macedonians, Albanians, Ottoman Turks, Serbs, Greek, Roma and other ethnic groups rub shoulders and bring their own cultural influences to the mix, including their folk music and traditional dances.

Macedonia's quarries produce marble which is so good that it is exported and then sold by the Italians as their own. There is some industry such as the production of steel and chemicals, but it is the crops that catch the eye as you travel around. In addition to fruits, vegetables and maize, there are tobacco plantations and extensive vineyards. Helped by the abundance of sun for much of the year, wine regions such as Tikves produce the most exquisite red and white wines. You'll also find the purest and sweetest of honeys on sale roadside, a must for taking home in your hold luggage, wrapped carefully. (As we discovered, broken honey jars can make quite a mess in a suitcase.)

The dramatic and extensive mountain terrain is penetrated by blissfully quiet trails for walking and horse riding, and more recently for mountain biking. The views are stunning. The wildlife includes the Eurasian Brown Bear, the Golden Jackal and the rare but beautiful Balkan Lynx. The country boasts a number of national parks and impressive caves for pot-holing. With mountain snow for much of the year, it also has its own ski resorts. Then there are the beautiful monasteries everywhere, fresco-adorned medieval churches and lovely small towns where you can chill out at friendly café bars.

Lake Ohrid, with its own airport, is the destination you will most likely find on Balkan travel guides. The beaches and clear waters are good for swimming. It has a 30km shoreline, scattered with ancient monasteries and ruined castles. The hills of Albania rise on the far side of the blue waters of what is claimed to be Europe's oldest lake. To the east, near the Greek and Bulgarian borders, is the smaller Dojran Lake which is becoming increasing popular as a festival location. Macedonia loves its festivals; there are festivals of film, comedy, folklore, traditional music, modern bands and even a wedding festival in the remote mountain village of Galicnik.

Macedonia's greatest attraction for tourists tends to be its scenery.

One highlight, though, is the ancient capital of Stobi. It is a site full of intriguing excavations; an engaging audio tour around Roman ruins brings alive a world full of synagogues, early churches, public baths, an amphitheatre and even an emperor's palace. When taking groups there, I like to muse on what life would have been like the day Paul first visited.

North Macedonia is cheap to visit from anywhere in Europe. Hotels are inexpensive by western standards, as is food and drink. It is also a long way down the tourism industry's rankings, so it remains a hidden gem, off the beaten track. Those who discover it are the lucky ones.

Appendix II: The Apostle Paul In Macedonia

A new vista opens up before him, raising the foreign traveller's spirits. The beautiful city in the valley below seems to shine at him through its marble walls and smile at him through its semi-circular amphitheatre.

With his companion forging on ahead, the older man has paused on the outskirts of Stobi, keen to rest his weary legs after the five-day walk. As he crouches down in the shade of a wall, he watches his hands disappear into the long loose sleeves of his robe. Then he lowers his turbaned head and takes a short nap. From a distance he looks like a pile of laundry.

On waking, the man takes out his time-worn map and spreads it out across his lap, pawing over it with some degree of wonder. The time in Thessalonica had been very fruitful; he had not had rocks thrown at him once. Travelling directly from one Roman provincial capital to another has added more detail to his vision. What if he can establish the Word of God here and plant a new centre for Christ's missionary work? Where might this emerging dream lead next? Perhaps north, to Scubi. As a shadow falls across him, he is lost in reflection,

"Or East to Tiberiopolis?" he murmurs.

His faithful young friend has returned with cool water, warm bread and moist figs. He has been gone longer than anticipated, having checked out where the Roman coins are minted.

"South to Heracles?" The older man's musings persist.

An excited voice demands his attention.

"Stobi has two synagogues."

Silas hands him a drink.

"West to where? Aah, you have figs. Good."

He looks up from the parchment and takes a long drink from the flask.

"Two synagogues, you say. Really? That's helpful. If we are thrown out of one, we go to the other."

Paul laughs.

***

Roman Macedonia had four provinces in the days of Jesus and the early church. Thessalonica was the capital of one province, Macedonia Prima (First Macedonia). Macedonia Salutaris (Wholesome Macedonia) covered most of what is now known as North Macedonia. This second Roman province included several prominent towns such as Scubi (now the capital Skopje), but the main city back then was Stobi, built on the former capital of the ancient kingdom of Paeonia.

The church in Europe started in Macedonia, when the Gospel first took hold in Luke's home town of Philippi. The churches mentioned in Paul's letters are towns and cities in First Macedonia (now Greece). However, it is clear from the book of Acts that Paul travelled extensively through all of the provinces of Macedonia, encouraging the believers where he had set up churches.[1]

The apostle also talks in his letter to the Roman church of his 'miracles and wonders' tour to Illyricum.[2] This was a region which stretched from modern-day Albania right up the Dalmatian coastline of Croatia. Paul's most direct route there would have been through Macedonia Salutaris. And if he travelled that way, there is no doubt he would have proclaimed the Good News about Christ at every opportunity.

There is still a strong verbal tradition today in North Macedonia that Paul did indeed visit. People are especially insistent that he preached in Stobi. Paul's mission strategy supports this possibility too. Arriving in a new area, he would head for its major cities. Where there were already Jewish communities, such as in Stobi, he would first try for an audience at the synagogue. When rejected, he turned to the non-Jews and established a church amongst them, initially in someone's home. Where successful, he might stay for a considerable time to grow and strengthen the church, before moving on.

His speaking ministry was accompanied by great signs and wonders. Paul had a phenomenal healing ministry. When Paul left an area, he would then encourage the churches by writing letters to them, a means of engaging a network of followers that he had learnt from his famous tutor Rabbi Gamaliel. None of the letters that were potentially written to Macedonia Salutaris survived.

Macedonia and the Macedonians are mentioned at least twenty times in the New Testament. They were an important part of Paul's church planting. It does indeed seem likely, therefore, that Paul himself set up the first churches in what is now North Macedonia.

If you travel to North Macedonia, do not miss out on looking round the ancient ruins of Stobi, just outside the small central town of Gradsko. Allow two hours minimum to walk around the extensive site, and as you walk around, try to visualise Paul or the first converts going about their daily life. Perhaps you could follow in Paul's footsteps and pray for this beautiful country, asking God to establish again his kingdom in this land of challenges.

References

1. Acts 20:1b-2

2. Romans 15:19

Appendix III: Mission Macedonia

Mission Macedonia is essentially two things.

First, Mission Macedonia is a focus for prayer. We meet in person and online to pray for the country of North Macedonia and its needs, for Jimmy and his team, for the churches and for the needs of individuals. We also seek to encourage each other to grow in Christ, in Holy Spirit gifting and in learning to see more miracles.

Second, Mission Macedonia is a registered charity with trustees. It works in partnership with the prayer group to raise finances and support the work out there, as well as publicising the needs of the Macedonian church to others. We are a small charity and have no overheads, so every donation goes in its entirety to support the work in Macedonia. We also have no big donors, so every donation is excitedly received.

Our stated charity purposes include:

Promote and advance all aspects of the Christian faith in Macedonia, through the holding of prayer meetings, lectures, conferences, public celebration of religious festivals, and producing or distributing Christian literature. Also to relieve hardship, and to promote and preserve good health by the provision of food, funds and support to benefit the homeless, elderly, disabled, single parent families and other persons in need.

One key aspect of our ministry is the annual New Hope conference that we started. This is a national event. We want it to be open to everyone and especially to be inclusive of the very poorest. Whilst those that can, give something towards the costs, the conference will not pay for itself, so the charity needs to find funding for each event. The main costs are the event venue, food, and transport from across the country.

Our vision statement for New Hope is to embrace the following:

- To encourage unity in the body of Christ.
- To nurture faith by encouragement through the scriptures.
- To love, bless and serve those who attend, in Jesus's name.
- To invite the Holy Spirit to bring healing.
- To celebrate people coming to salvation.
- To rejoice in lives transformed by God.
- To worship the Father, Son and Holy Spirit.

If you wish to get involved or support us in any way, you can contact us by email at missionmacedonia@outlook.com

We send out periodic newsletters and you can add your name to our distribution list by sending us your email address and by giving us permission to add you.

We also have a Mission Macedonia Facebook page where we post news and prayer requests. https://www.facebook.com/mission.macedonia

If you wish to support our work financially, please send a bank transfer using the following account details:

Mission Macedonia, Lloyds Bank sort-code 30-98-90, account number 20782660

If you then email us and tell us what you have sent, we can thank you for the donation.

Proceeds from this book will support the work of Mission Macedonia.

Appendix IV: Useful Books

Among the many books about miracles and healing, here are my top ten that I found particularly inspiring or practically useful:

Norman Grubb, *Rees Howells Intercessor* (Guildford: Lutterworth Press 1983, 8th impression)

Heidi and Rolland Baker, *Birthing the Miraculous* (Grand Rapids, Chosen Books 2007)

John Eckhardt, *Prayers that Rout Demons* (Lake Mary, Charisma House 2008)

Jack Moraine, *Healing Ministry* (Choctaw, HGM Publishing 2010)

Jerry Trousdale, *Miraculous Movements* (Nashville, Thomas Nelson 2012)

Jordan Seng, *Miracle Work* (Madison, Inter Varsity Press 2013)

Jeannie Morgan, *Our hands, his healings* (Oxford, Monarch Books 2014)

John Peters, *Third Person* (Maidstone, River Publishing & Media Ltd 2017)

Robby Dawkins, *Do greater things* (Grand Rapids, Chosen Books 2018)

Craig S Keener, *Miracles Today* (Grand Rapids, Baker Academic 2021)

Appendix V: Allaboutjesus.info

Jesus was not born simply in order to die a sacrificial death. At 30 years old, the son (or rather, adopted son) of a carpenter, already immersed in his spiritual Father's Word, stopped his manual work and went on the road for three glorious years, teaching about the kingdom of God and doing extraordinary things. Those short years have changed millions of lives and their impact grows all the time.

If you want a resource that will help you know more about what Jesus did and what it all means, then please check out my website **www.allaboutjesus.info.**

I have put together a time line on the life of Jesus. This links to the gospel passages, but also to videos I have created on the different aspects of his life. These cover the miracles, parables, sayings and the special life events of Jesus. The videos consist of talks accompanied by still images which change every few seconds. They each last between 15 and 20 minutes and are aimed at both teaching and inspiring you. Ideally, you can sit down at lunch in a café or works canteen with your headphones on and make them part of your routine.

If you are a small group leader, you can show the videos to your group as part of a discussion around a gospel passage. If you are a preacher or church leader, hard pushed for time, then I have also attached all the sermon notes that accompany each talk, and these can be taken as the starting point for your own preaching.

There is also an 'All about Jesus' account in YouTube which can be found by searching **'kevin elliott allaboutjesus.info'**, or can be entered via the allaboutjesus website home page.

The YouTube account is useful as it has a number of playlists for the different types of talks, such as a playlist on the miracles of Jesus. There are also extras linked to the YouTube account including 3-minute versions of some talks and a playlist of videos about the work of Mission Macedonia. One of these is an inspiring hour-long YouTube documentary which follows the very first mission trip in 2017, called *Miracles in Macedonia*. It is the perfect complement to this book, providing the visual backdrop for the journey that we have just taken together. It really is not to be missed! You can find it easily, but the direct link is:

https://youtu.be/JhaJAPU6abk

To get daily updates and encouragement, you can also follow **allaboutjesus.info** on Instagram.

All the resources are free to use, so please give them a try.

Appendix VI: Team Testimonies

My trip was amazing. The whole week's activities were filled with the Holy Spirit at work in us. I saw and experienced miracles that I would not have believed if I didn't see it for myself. The trip had a profound effect on me. It changed me, as a follower of Jesus Christ. All honour and glory to God.

Doreen Dyer

The prayer time at New Hope blew me away. It was almost overwhelming. People were trying to jump the queue. People were running and pushing in, and I found myself getting pushed further and further back. We were in pairs to start with, and we couldn't cope in pairs so had to pray individually. And people were just being healed, in seconds in some instances.

Jason Bryant

It's been an amazing journey. I am supremely privileged to be a part of it and one of many sent to pick up where the apostle Paul left off in Macedonia.

Tracey Taylor

One day, I heard God telling me that I will go around the world and make films for him about what the Holy Spirit was doing. I had no idea what that would look like and told no-one. Two weeks later,

Kevin asked me if I would film his trip to Macedonia. I went and it was a wonderful experience. I returned six years later to film the sequel.

Mario Ivanov

I was out of my comfort zone, and I had no idea what I was doing, yet I saw miracle after miracle after miracle. It was super-intensive but life-changing. It has reminded me of just how loving, powerful and active our Father God is. I didn't think I would be particularly useful going to a country I knew little about, with no prior experience of overseas mission, but God used my availability not my ability. I was completely reliant on God's strength.

Simeon Elliott

Mission trips to Macedonia have given me the space and opportunities to grow my giftings from God in ways that aren't afforded to me back in England.

Stephen Selby

We loved being part of an open-air outreach event, helping a pastor reach out to a Roma village. It was the first evangelism in this area, and we saw more than twenty respond to the salvation call. Villagers then came forward for healing prayer ministry. It was a joy to all be working together building God's kingdom

Jono and Heather Cox

My time in North Macedonia has been eye opening. God has shown up in amazing ways and time and time again He has continued to surprise me. Out of his great love for the people of North Macedonia, I have seen many people healed and saved into His kingdom. God has multiplied our efforts far beyond anything that I could have ever imagined.

Ellie Grice

We want to thank and glorify God, that he was willing to use the two of us for his kingdom work in Macedonia. We had to step out of the boat, then trust and let God lead.

Ian and Sue Packer

Wow, all glory to God! It's been amazing to be used by God in powerful ways. All I had to do is to show up and to be available - God did the rest! He spoke through me and touched others through me. He healed others through me. I am amazed that he would use me. It was incredible seeing God move and engaging with Him. He is good.

Eva Ivanov

It was an honour to join in. There is something delightfully raw and 'New Testament-like' about the mission endeavours of Jimmy and his troops. So much evidence of heartfelt commitment to the cause of Jesus and the growth of his Kingdom. So much love for the people, especially the poor, in this beautiful but tormented nation. So much conviction that the power of the gospel does indeed transform lives, families and communities. And what self-sacrificial dedication among these servants. It was a privilege for a while, to worship and work alongside. All power to their ministry.

Tim Grew

Appendix VII: Acknowledgements

I want to thank everyone in my story. Without you there would not be a story to tell.

Love and thanks to my mother Grace, who was fundamental in giving me the right environment to find and develop my faith. She taught me to pray daily, read the Bible daily, and go to church. Thanks to all my family for putting up with me. Love you. I am also indebted to those who have prayed for me, many of whom I will never know.

I owe a debt of gratitude to Brother Jimmy, Simon Polikarp, for the many opportunities to minister alongside him in Macedonia, despite my naiveties and shortfalls. I also want to thank his team, past and present, for always embracing me in their love. Similarly, I want to thank Bishop Earnest and his team of the Kericho Diocese in Kenya, for taking me in and enabling me to serve amongst them there, and to Pastor Ben Nengo for inviting me to Mombasa.

I want to thank Cheddar Baptist Church where I grew up for my spiritual nurture, then both Charlton Kings Baptist Church and Highbury Congregational Church (where I did most of my youth-work and preaching) for the opportunities to serve and grow in my faith. Thanks also to the leaders and many friends at Trinity Cheltenham, for accepting and helping both myself and Mission Macedonia; in particular I would like to thank Pastor Tim Grew for his sustained support and understanding.

Those who have journeyed with me, I salute you. Through my early years, my youthwork days and my engineering jobs, it has been a privilege to walk alongside so many of you. We have shared our lives and learnt on route, shedding a few tears but also having a lot of fun.

To all those who have invested in Mission Macedonia since 2016, a huge thank you. Jobbo and Jason, thanks for getting us so well established. Thanks Ian, Sue, Ellie, Mario, Eva, Stephen, Sinead, Trudie, Tracey, Heather, Jono, Katrina and Jacqui who have made the prayer meetings and prophecy groups a joy to be at, and for your huge contribution to our mission trips.

Thanks to all the others who have come out on any of our trips. You were great. Thanks to Derek too, who has stepped into help me with the charity finances and proof reading of this book, and the others I roped in for comment. A big thank you to my friend Dave Waters for his kind words, and to Simon Guillebaud for his inspiration and encouragement.

Richard Coton, my editor, gets a special mention for wrestling this book into a new and much better shape. Richard: no matter how often I winced as you scythed through successive drafts of the text, I really appreciate what you've done.

Finally, thank you Jesus for

saving my life,

being my everything

and teaching me to see miracles.

I love finding a hidden unlisted track on a CD (sometimes called 'an easter egg') or staying to the end of the film credits and seeing an extra scene. It is like an unexpected reward for the most persistent. So for those of you who have kept going and got this far... this is for you.

The Easter Egg

I had wondered at the time what I had done with that brightly painted hard-boiled egg, gifted me on the Easter Sunday of the 2023 mission trip. Now at home, as I emptied out everything from the last of the six compartments of my shoulder bag, it unexpectedly rolled out from the bottom of a deep crease.

Over the last week, we had seen God continually moving in power, saving, blessing and healing.

That bag had been everywhere, from our street evangelism in the ancient northern town of Kratovo, to the serene Lake Dojran on the Greek border. It had been thrown around whilst travelling to a second evangelism event in the central rural hamlet of Peshirovo then onwards to the hard-edged southern city of Prilep and its nearby rubbish-laden Roma communities. Things had been constantly pushed into and out of those pockets. The egg was hidden there all the time.

Messy

New Hope 2023 had moved to Gradsko Town Hall after we had lost our use of the Gemidgii stadium in Veles. Crowds had quickly filled all the seats in the large white box-like room, lit by huge windows adorned with fading red curtains. Soon people were standing down the sides. Then another coach load arrived. We had just a small UK team of five, as a number of potential volunteers had dropped out. I knew many Macedonians would be coming to New

Hope for healing so we would need to do things differently in order to cope.

Stephen, our keyboard player, got a word from God on the way there that the event would not go as planned. It would be messy and we were just to roll with it. The warning was indeed helpful; during the middle of my talk, without any notice, I was ushered off stage to do a local TV interview outside the front doors. I left Stephen alone on the large stage unsure what was happening. Fifteen minutes later, I returned to find the platform now full of people circling around two traditional folk musicians in an energetic Macedonian dance.

I eventually got into my stride again, incorporating a ministry time within the talk. We called out those who had pains and sickness in their bodies or minds, and I prayed over them from the stage, whilst Stephen played prophetically inspired music over them. The Holy Spirit descended across the hall. I later asked for a show of hands for those that had felt their pain go, or felt they had been healed of sickness etc. Hands went up all across the room. It was hard to count them, but there were a lot.

I continued preaching the Easter Story, declaring the resurrection life in Jesus, then handed on to Jimmy who wrapped up and gave a salvation appeal. Again, the scale of positive response was hard to take in. We had not realised how many were at New Hope for the first time. It looked like nearly a third of the crowd had stood up. Jimmy, not quite believing his eyes, re-iterated that just those making a first-time commitment should stand. No-one sat down, and even more stood up!

When the event had finished, people pressed in on us for more healing. One man in a bright orange jacket, who had enthusiastically given his life to Jesus was now talking with Ellie, Mario and Eva. In a terrifying dream some time ago, he had seen Satan and when he woke up, he had suffered partial sight loss and so needed strong glasses. He was also experiencing hearing problems and stiffness in his fingers. They prayed for him, breaking off the dream's curse. He took off his glasses and proclaimed with joy that he could now see clearly. His eyesight was fully restored. After more prayer the feeling and movement in his fingers returned and his hearing improved. In my queue, I was surprised to be enthusiastically engaged by a lady in typical Muslim clothes, who wanted prayer in the Holy Spirit against cancer in her body, and for her child's fever to go.

Every prayer our team prayed that day brought its own testimony of healing or blessing or both. Similar experiences on previous trips did not at all diminish the joy and amazement of being used by God in this way.

A Bit Like The Egg

I now looked more carefully at the painted egg that had travelled with me around North Macedonia. The shell was broken in places and it was slightly crushed. Surprisingly, though, it was still otherwise intact despite all it had been through.

Our team was a bit like the egg. They had been through a lot. There had been a number of spiritual attacks. Just before they had set off to Macedonia, Mario and Eva's house had survived a fire that had started in their under-stair cupboard after a battery on an electric unicycle had exploded at night. During the trip, three of the team had endured stomach bugs, and Stephen sprained his ankle badly. They all kept going. Then Ellie had returned from the airport at 3.30am to find her kitchen sink had been leaking onto the floor whilst she was away.

Now at home, I checked in with myself. I did not feel the same spiritual oppression that I sometimes experienced following a trip. Everything had gone so well. Yet at that moment I did feel a bit numb, unsure of how to process it all. We had all been stretched and seen so many miracles. Yet, I was having difficulty this time in grasping the full scale of what had just happened.

How do I internalise these things? What are the next steps from here? When people politely ask, *'How was Macedonia?'* where do I find the expected handful of adequate words? How will I feel, when I share testimony and get those blank looks of unbelief, since so many are strangely unexcited and unmoved by what I have said?

Regretfully, I lobbed the Easter egg into the bin. It had missed out on its main two purposes of being rolled or eaten. But then I smiled. We may get cracked and damaged but Jesus would never throw us away. The adventure will just keep rolling forward and nourishing our souls.

Our emotions help us navigate our experiences but are fickle and ever changing, influenced by a whole range of factors. Our feelings may be affected by whether people believe our stories or not, but the facts of what just happened will not change. And God has plenty more for us to do. God's word and truth are constant; they are the bedrock for our decision making, not our emotions.

As long as we continue to make ourselves available, no matter how we feel on any given day, he will continue to work out his purposes in us and through us.

We are in this together, on team Jesus, and together we will see miracles.

Thank you, Lord.

Milton Keynes UK
Ingram Content Group UK Ltd.
UKHW010232090224
437353UK00004B/8